PATHFINDER DRESSAGE

PENNY HILLSDON

PATHFINDER DRESSAGE

The Philosophy and Training Techniques
of the World's Top Trainers

J. A. ALLEN LONDON

British Library cataloguing in Publication Data
A catalogue record for this book is available from the British Library

ISBN 0.85131.745.6

Published in Great Britain in 2000 by
J. A. Allen an imprint of Robert Hale Ltd.,
Clerkenwell House, 45–47 Clerkenwell Green,
London EC1R 0HT

Artwork on pages 3, 5, 9, 166 and 167 by Judy Lowther.
Line illustrations on pages 84 and 85 by Christine Bousfield.

Front cover photograph of Ellen Bontje riding Silvano N © Guido Recki.
All text photographs © Bob Langrish, except for the photograph of
Michel Assouline on page 73 © Expo Life, the photograph on page 17 © the Spanish Riding School,
the photograph on page 63 (personal property of Franz Rochowansky),
and the photograph on page 168 (personal property of Sylvia Loch).

Extracts from other publications quoted and accredited within the text are
all the copyright of the original publications and are reproduced with permission.
In this respect, the author and publishers acknowledge with thanks
permissions from the following:

British Dressage, for the extracts on p 15
Dressage Magazine, for the extracts on pp 7–8, 72, 74
Dressage Today, for the extracts on p 18
Half Halt Press, for the extracts on p 156
Charles Harris, for the extracts on pp 166–167
Horse and Hound, for the extracts on pp 74, 165
The Classical Riding Club newsletter for extracts on ps 170
The Sportsman's Press for the extracts on pp 150, 165

All other extracts quoted are taken from titles published by J.A. Allen

Design by Paul Saunders
Typeset by Textype Typesetters, Cambridge
Colour processing by Tenon & Polert Colour Processing Ltd., Hong Kong
Printed in Hong Kong by Dah Hua International Printing Press Co. Ltd.

Contents

Dedication   viii
Acknowledgements   ix

1 THE LEGACY OF DRESSAGE   1

An Historical Overview   3
Classical Icons   4
  The Spanish Riding School of Vienna; De la Gueriniéré's
  Perspective on Shoulder-In; The French School
Dressage for the Twenty-first Century   12

2 MIRRORS OF CLASSICAL DRESSAGE   17

LESSON ONE · **Training with Vicki Thompson**   21
Position of the Rider   21
  General Guidelines to a Good Position; The Seat; The Legs;
  The Shoulders, Arms and Hands
Lunge Lessons   25
  Lunge Lessons for the Novice Rider; Lunge Lessons for the Advanced Rider
Direct Transitions, Half-Transitions and Half-Halts   35
  Direct Transitions; Half-Transitions; Half-Halts
Figure Riding   37
  Turns and Circles
Guide to the Working Gaits   39
Guide to Collecting the Gaits   41
Guide to Lengthening the Gaits   43
  Lengthening Steps in Trot; Extending the Steps
Introducing Lateral Work   45

Shoulder-Fore; Shoulder-In; Travers

Developing Lateral Work   52

Half-Pass; The Pirouettes

Advancing the Canter   57

Simple Changes; Single Flying Changes

The First Steps of Piaffe   59

Vicki Thompson's Training Tips   60

Vicki Thompson's Profile   62

3   FLAGS OF MODERN DRESSAGE   65

4   THE GERMAN WAY   76

LESSON TWO · **Training with Ferdi Eilberg**   76

The German Scales of Training   76

Scale 1: *Losgelassenheit*; Scale 2: Rhythm; Scale 3: Contact;

Scale 4: *Schwung*; Scale 5: Straightness; Scale 6: Collection

Training the Young Horse   89

The Half-Halts   91

The Movements   92

Shoulder-In; Other Lateral Work; Extension; Canter Pirouettes;

Flying Changes; Piaffe and Passage

Ferdi Eilberg's Training Tips   103

Ferdi Eilberg's Profile   104

5   THE DUTCH WAY   111

LESSON THREE · **Training with Bert Rutten**   111

Training an Elementary Horse   114

Training a Grand Prix Horse   117

Bert Rutten's Profile   120

LESSON FOUR · **Training with Jane Bredin**   121

Simplicity   122

Time-Factor   123

Training for Competition

Training by Opposites   124

Submission   125

The Submission Point; Equal Pressure on Both Reins;

Riding the Horse in a Round Shape; General Information on Submission;

Flexing; Bending

The Aids   131

Light off the Legs; The Hands; The Seat; Half-Halts

The Working Movements   134

Corners and Circles; Working Shoulder-In; Working Travers;

Working Half-Pass; Working Pirouettes; Working Flying Changes;

Piaffe and Passage; Fine-Tuning

Muscle Power, Connection and Balance   144

Summary   145

Jane Bredin's Profile   145

6 DRESSAGE SIDELINES   150

LESSON FIVE · **Lungeing**   150

LESSON SIX · **The Spanish Way – Work In-Hand**   155

Starting The Horse   156

Lungeing; Starting the Ridden Work

Techniques for Work In-Hand   158

7 CULTIVATING BRAIN POWER   162

LESSON SEVEN · **The Classical Seat of the Spanish Riding
School as described by Charles Harris**   163

LESSON EIGHT · **The Classical Dressage Seat of the Iberian
Schools as described by Sylvia Loch**   168

The Great Debate: Other Trainers' Views   171

HIGHWAYS TO DRESSAGE   175

Index   179

*This book is dedicated to
my family with love and thanks*

ACKNOWLEDGEMENTS

There are so many people to thank for making *Pathfinder Dressage* a reality; it would be impossible to list them all – but to you all I send my most heart-warm thanks.

The Lessons have involved talented trainers in time, energy and work; most particularly Vicki Thompson, Ferdi Eilberg, Bert Rutten and Jane Bredin. They have given so much of their knowledge, gained through many years of hard work and determination, and it is very humbling to realise that this was done without financial reward, but to help others get joy out of dressage. Many thanks.

Thanks also to First Chief Rider Arthur Kottas of the Spanish Riding School of Vienna, Michel Assouline, Conrad Schumacher, Herr Franz Rochowansky, Charles Harris, the late Dr Reiner Klimke, Paul Fielder, Peter Maddison-Greenwell, Sylvia Loch, Jane Kidd and Paul Belasik.

A special thanks has to go to my friend and colleague, Bob Langrish for supplying such superb photographs. Special thanks also to Judy Lowther for her beautiful illustrations.

Much appreciation goes to the editor, Martin Diggle. His keen eye zoomed in on any unclear words or passages and his astute observations added merit to the book. Thanks also to Paul Saunders, the designer, for giving *Pathfinder Dressage* such a clean, fresh image.

The publisher Caroline Burt deserves a medal. She has remained very enthusiastic and always excited about the next book. Thanks Caroline.

CHAPTER 1

The Legacy of Dressage

The legacy of dressage has been handed down through thousands of years and myriad cultures. Over the centuries many techniques have been blended together in a universal melting pot where differences and similarities evolve. *Pathfinder Dressage* explores some of the world's established and successful methods of training; it explains theories but focuses on the practical and readers are 'taught' in lesson format so they can emulate the advice when teaching their own horses.

Sometimes dressage is spurred to advance by the arrival of genius riders and trainers. Their talents feed the Nile of existing dressage and elevate it to greater and greater heights. Uniformity should never stifle originality, imagination and natural ability. Dressage would be poorer for adopting such a stringent, unyielding path. Imagine François de la Guérinière being told in the eighteenth century, 'Sorry, the shoulder-in has never been performed before so dressage cannot accommodate this suppling exercise!' Surely such a dogmatic attitude would have killed ingenuity and perhaps destroyed the birth of dressage thousands of years ago. However, the profusion of so many training methods can confuse. We must understand that there is a 'bedrock' of dressage; a constant, if winding, 'main river' of principles into which further streams of knowledge continue to converge. If we comprehend this then the door of understanding will open.

Logically, the constituent parts of dressage can never be identical. All dimensions would have to be exact: trainers would have to be isolated in an environment where they were taught in exactly the same way as preceding trainers; they would have to train horses of identical genes, conformation, movement and temperament. The Spanish Riding School of Vienna is the closest example of 'identical' dressage: the purity and exactness of master and student being played as an art form so that each represents the other. This nearness, this exactness is the absolute reason why The Spanish Riding School has a role in the modern world. It is a pure example of excellence and a source of original form – a reference point echoing back to the teachings of Xenophon. But outside the walls of these Classical ideals, reproduction dressage does not exist. This surely is its fascination. Dressage is a living entity like music or singing which can be created, originated, replicated taken to the heights of genius, follow normal standards or live as an exciting Olympic sport but – thankfully – dressage can never be reproduced.

Just appreciate the qualities and dedication needed to create top-class trainers and riders - the skills, the talents, the flashes of luck needed to carry these élite to the top grades of dressage. Access to the very top is even more difficult. The rider must be experienced with dressage horses from top bloodlines; must have observed and ridden countless horses at all levels of training from Novice to Grand Prix; and must have opportunities to discuss training techniques with a person of superior knowledge. There is also the need for oodles of talent! Compute these ingredients of excellence and it becomes apparent why there are so few really top-class riders and trainers. These élite shower us with good examples to cherish. Some are quoted in *Pathfinder Dressage* and have given their advice to help all 'out there' aspiring to better dressage. How a rider trains is based upon individual background, interpretation of a particular 'school', and disposal of individual abilities. For example, a rider may remain close to the methods first taught, or be innovative and develop new ways, or add on existing techniques from another source. All of these factors proliferate different ways of training. This partly explains the rapid growth of dressage, but after the Second World War its popularity spiralled ever more upward – this being a time when cultural barriers began breaking down.

Two points remain cast in stone. First, from quality comes quality – the very crux of excellence in dressage – and second, dressage encompasses the whole spectrum from the beginnings of training a horse (i.e. backing the youngster) to the ultimate state of horsemanship – Grand Prix (competition) dressage and Haute Ecole dressage. Skills are passed on from Master to Master and, luckily for dressage, much accumulated knowledge has been signposted by books, sculptures, paintings and illustrations, and now this store of information can be further enhanced by modern forms of communication such as photography, videos, films and computers. Naturally, the person receiving any imparted knowledge must always be open to the realities of miscommunication, such as misprints, misexplanations, language differences and photographs taken at the wrong moment to miscontrue correctness. An 'eye', or instinctive built-in detector for correctness is an essential component for any serious student or trainer of dressage. A good trainer will always impart an open-minded, intellectual attitude to the students.

AN HISTORICAL OVERVIEW

Today's dressage derives its position of authority from a backbone of history that originated in ancient Greece. The Parthenon stone carvings, created about 450 BC, show horses in piaffe, passage and the levade. We can glimpse the Greek's

humane methods of training from a book written around 400 BC by the cavalry officer, Xenophon. He said, 'If you desire to handle a good war-horse so as to make his action the more magnificent and striking, you must refrain from pulling at his mouth with the bit as well as from spurring and whipping him.' He continues 'If you teach your horse to go with a light hand on the bit, and yet to hold his head well up and to arch his neck, you will be making him do just what the animal himself glories and delights in.' And again, 'The horse's mouth must not be checked too harshly, so that he will toss his head, nor too gently for him to feel it. The moment he acknowledges it and begins to raise his neck, give him the bit. And in everything else, as I have insisted over and over again, the horse should be rewarded as long as he behaves well.' He also wrote, 'The one great precept and practice in using a horse is this – never deal with him when you are in a fit of passion. A fit of passion is a thing that has no foresight in it, and so we often have to rue the day when we gave way to it.' Xenophon's teachings of kindness and compassion towards the horse fit the modern dressage rider very well. (A modern translation of Xenophon's book *Art of Horsemanship* is published by J. A. Allen & Co).

It is too horrendous to imagine, but Xenophon's enlightened thinking nearly got extinguished forever! In fact, you could say, dressage died for the next 2,000 years, but underwent a rebirth in the sixteenth century owing to the Italian nobleman Federico Grisone. His book *Ordine di Cavalcare* picked up the reins of Xenophon's teachings. He studied Xenophon's book and quoted him almost word for word on the seat and aids of the rider. Grisone, who is widely recognised as the 'father of the art of equitation', established the first riding academy in Naples in 1532. One of his best pupils, Pignatelli, later became Director of the riding academy and imparted his knowledge to other great riders such as Antoine de Pluvinel and Salomon de la Broue. In the meantime, two of Grisone's students, Paolo d'Quino and Vargas, introduced dressage to Spain, while Georg Englehard von Löhneissen spread the word to Germany.

A disciple of Pignatelli named Saint Antoine travelled to England and influenced William Cavendish, Duke of Newcastle. In the aftermath of the Civil War, he founded a riding school in Antwerp and wrote *The Method and Novel Ways of Training Horses*, before returning to England after the Restoration.

Antoine de Pluvinel (1555–1620) was a great influence in France. He tempered medieval training methods by treating the horse with humanity (which was contrary to the ideas of that time). De Pluvinel believed that a horse should be taught by rewards of titbits, praise and petting and, like Xenophon, that the horse should be allowed to think. He understood dressage as a close bond between rider and horse. He had a profound influence on the art of dressage and laid the foundation stones for that genius of dressage, François Robichon de la Guérinière. Today, the principles of Guérinière's teachings are followed almost unaltered by the Spanish Riding School of Vienna. In 1716 Guérinière opened a riding academy in Versailles and his training methods founded another great School that still exists, The School of Cavalry at Saumur.

However, during the eighteenth and nineteenth centuries, a succession of European wars took their toll and the main seats of dressage were seen only in France and Vienna. Sooner than feared the French Revolution scattered the remnants of their knowledge and the Napoleonic wars desecrated most of the riding academies of Europe. The Spanish Riding School of Vienna remained as an oasis, flying its standard for all to see.

CLASSICAL ICONS

Dressage was originally conceived by the sword and through the ages the icons of dressage have been severely battered by the effects of war. But, despite the barbarities, dressage was preserved. Let us look briefly at those institutions that have, by their continuing influence, helped dressage to keep moving forwards.

The Spanish Riding School of Vienna

Ask most people what they understand as 'Classical' and they say, 'The Spanish Riding School of Vienna' – the ethos of the School is imbedded in the psyche of horse lovers all over the world. Its influence is strengthened by its distinction of being the only School to survive and prosper since its inception in the sixteenth century.

Despite potentially mongrelising influences that could have reshaped and altered its ideals, the Spanish Riding School of Vienna remains untarnished; a pure light in a world of swirling changes; a Mecca for all to look up to, glamorous but uncluttered by mystical dogma. Its hallmark is simplicity, and herein lies its true beauty.

Sceptics have questioned its role in the modern world. To explain this, a quote is taken from one of the School's publications:

> If you ask what purpose is served by an institution such as that represented by the Spanish Riding School – a question of great topical interest, especially in this age of mechanization, ostentatious display and blaring publicity in nearly all sectors of life – the answer is: art and breeding. Or you might put breeding first, and art second. Actually it does not matter one way or another in this realm of the centaurs: Man and animal are fused into a single artistic personality that develops according to its own laws and displays its beauty regardless of publicity. A vision of beauty is made real by a visionary; it is imparted to the onlookers as lightly, as effortlessly as though it were a leaf floating down in the fall breeze.

From *The Spanish Riding School of Vienna*, edited by Bundesministerium Für Land-Und Forstwirtschaft, Vienna 1970.

Tom Sewell, The founder of Training the Teachers of Tomorrow, a Teachers' Training Trust in England, says; 'Good training is therapeutic for both horse and rider: this applies at all levels, whether Novice or Grand Prix. The basic goal of training is to make the horse easier to ride and more comfortable in his work. Only the fully developed athlete is able to show the full range of movement.'

Chief Riders of the Spanish Riding School are regarded as gods and individual references go back centuries. To mention a few: Paul von Schafer appointed in 1731, the outstanding rider Maximilian von Weyrother, and in the twentieth Century Colonel Hans Handler, Colonel Podhajsky, Brigadier General Albrecht and the present and youngest-ever Herr Arthur Kottas. Tom Sewell wrote, 'To become an *Oberbereiter* (Chief Rider) or – in the case of Kottas, First Chief Rider – you need more than talent, you need genius.'

The history of the School reads like Tolstoy's *War and Peace*. Upheavals, threats to survival, impossible odds thwarted, and its continuation is owed to the bravery and integrity of individual riders – this history is etched into the walls of the School's buildings and runs in the genes of the Lipizzaner horses. This breed was founded in 1580, with nine Spanish stallions and twenty-four mares. It has five principal stallion lines: Pluto (1765), Conversano (1767), Neapolitan (1779), Siglavy (1810) and Maestoso (1819). The Lipizzaner's conformation and temperament make it particularly suitable for dressage. Herr Arthur Kottas says about

The Spanish Riding School of Vienna on display

Lipizzaner in levade

the Lipizzaner horse, 'He has such a willing temperament. They are such good characters and very obliging and wanting to please the rider.'

Talking about his role as the First Chief Rider of the School, Arthur Kottas says, 'It's a dream come true, if you are a rider it is the greatest achievement.' Talking with Pauline Norton in an article for *Dressage* magazine, he made the following points:

The Spanish School riders must love animals and have complete dedication. It is not difficult to join, but is more difficult to stay. You must have a good feeling for the horses. A rider must not only be capable of riding a trained horse, but able to train a young stallion up to Grand Prix level.

To aspiring dressage riders he says:

Training, training and more training. Find yourself the best trainer you can afford and choose a horse who is right for your level of riding. Ideally, a novice rider should learn to ride on a well-trained horse. Of course, it is possible for a novice horse and novice rider to work together, but it will take much longer and they will make more mistakes.

I always say, there is no theory without practice and no practice without theory. If you are working on a particular movement with your horse and your theory is not working, then you must go away and restudy your theory to find out why it is not working. Do not just keep repeating an exercise if the horse does not understand.

De la Guérinière's Perspective on Shoulder-in

As explained, the Spanish Riding School of Vienna still follows the principles of great Masters and particularly Guérinière. He is credited with having created that great suppling, straightening and strengthening movement, the shoulder-in. In his book, *Ecole de Cavalerie*, Guérinière wrote about shoulder-in:

The circle is not the best means of suppling the shoulders, since a thing constrained and under its own weight cannot be light . . . The shoulder cannot be rendered supple if the inside hind leg is not advanced closely to the outside hind leg during the exercise.

He explained when to start teaching shoulder-in:

When a horse can trot freely, then, in both directions in a circle and on a straight line; when it can walk those same figures with a quiet and even step; and when it has become accustomed to executing halts and half-halts, and to carrying the head to the inside, it must then be taken at a slow and relatively extended gait along the wall and placed so that the haunches delineate one line and the shoulders another.

He listed the benefits of shoulder-in:

1. In the first place, the exercise supples the shoulders.

2. The shoulder-in prepares a horse to be put on its haunches, and learns in consequence to bend its hocks under itself; this is what is called being on the haunches.

3. This same exercise disposes a horse to move away from the leg . . . which it must be able to do in order to move sideways with ease.

He adds his observations of the movement; 'I regard the shoulder-in as an indispensable aid in achieving flexibility of the shoulders and the ability to cross the legs easily one over the other. A perfection which all horses must have if they are to be called well-formed and well trained.'

The French School

The Saumur Cadre Noir lives as another icon of Classical excellence. The School was founded in the Renaissance years after two Pignatelli students, Antoine de Pluvinel and Salomon de la Broue, introduced academic equitation into France. Until the eighteenth century it acted as the role model throughout Europe. Unfortunately the School was destroyed by the French Revolution and not resurrected until 1815, and then (initially) for only fifteen years. However, its traditions lived on through the riders and grooms, and it was through them that the original Cadre Noir spirit could be rekindled. One of its famous riders General Decarpentry (1878–1956) wrote:

It is therefore only by a somewhat tenuous thread of indirect transmission that the School of Saumur was linked in its beginnings to the School of Versailles. In those circumstances, it was inevitable that Baucher's brilliant achievements would divert devotees away from academic equitation towards the artistic conception of this Master, with its qualities and its faults, and the Manège became 'baucheriste', under the direction of Commandant de Novital . . . The School, however had an essential mission which had to take precedence over all considerations of tradition: this was to establish, to fix and to elaborate a Military Equitation, because Saumur is a Cavalry School rather than an Academy of Equestrian Art. Count d'Aure devoted himself to this task and in this he was remarkably successful.

Decarpentry goes on to explain how the standards were re-established:

The riding masters were free to use the methods of their earlier education; for instance, Guerin used those of Baucher, and Montigny those of Vienna, where he had been a student and a Master, and they all upheld a Classical correction and elegance of which the Riding Master in Chief was a shining example. Thus, although it remained confined to the 'Cadre' of the Manège, artistic equitation lived on at the Cavalry School.

And he says of one Master's influence over the standards:

Finally, General L'Hotte, faithful successor of D'Aure as regards the education of the students, himself practised on his own horses the highest difficulties of the art and succeeded in pouring into the mould of the Versailles tradition the most refined inventions of Baucher's genius. He was later, in his book *Questions Equestres* to give a corpus of doctrine to that modern French School that owes almost everything to him.

General Decarpentry was, himself, a man of outstanding dressage achievements. He was the grandson of one Baucher's students and he served in the Cadre Noir for fourteen years, eight (1933–9) as Riding Master. He was an international dressage judge, and on some occasions presided over the jury of the Fédération Equestre Internationale (FEI). He wrote many dressage books, his best known being *Academic Equitation*.

In 1829, the Ecuyer en Chef Jean-Baptiste Cordier had started the influence of a Charter of Equitation. After the First World War, international competitors were promoted by the Saumur and this devolution from dressage to other equestrian disciplines, particularly show jumping, impacted upon the direction of the School. One of the School's five main aims is: 'Through the work of the Cadre Noir to maintain the splendid quality and traditions of French equitation.' The 'cross-over' has brought with it an array of facilities probably incomparable anywhere worldwide.

A man of considerable dressage experience is Michel Assouline. He went to the

National Equestrian School (NES) at Saumur in 1977 for two years and was taught by the present Chief Rider, Colonel Laporte Du Theil. He says, 'In France the riding clubs gave everybody the chance to go forwards to the Saumur for selection (they went to train and qualify for the *Bereiter* examination). The selection was tough and took place over three days. You were judged on a dressage test, show jumping, cross-country riding and a written exam. Only about 25 per cent of the hopeful students passed to go onto the School.'

Michel says of his time at the School: 'When I joined it was in the process of building new facilities. I was based in town at the old-fashioned buildings, but they have such a charm of their own. I really enjoyed it. I was taught a lot on the retired carousel and quadrille horses [former display horses used as schoolmasters]. It was such a good experience to ride such well-trained horses. What I particularly like about the Saumur is they train so many different breeds of horses through to Haute Ecole dressage. For example, breeds such as the Warmbloods, pure Thoroughbreds and Selle Français horses. The old Masters learnt so many good tips about handling "hot-blooded" horses, and knowing their techniques helps train the modern sports horse. What I gained from the School has really helped me produce horses for dressage competition.'

The élite riders of the Saumur belong to the Cadre Noir and every July they display their excellence in a dressage performance including airs above the ground and the quadrille. The Cadre Noir's history is steeped in talent and it has shared its

The Cadre Noir on display (and on following page)

knowledge openly with many influential riders of the past, such as Guérinière, Baucher, Fillis and M. Saint-Fort Paillard. Elegance ripples through the Cadre Noir and those who practise its traditions.

DRESSAGE FOR THE TWENTY-FIRST CENTURY

Many people today refute ideas of exclusivity, which in the past had been the hallmarks of dressage. Nowadays, dressage has spread to thousand upon thousands of enthusiasts and it continues to be a fast-growing sport.

Protecting the ethos of competition dressage are some special 'guardians' of dressage. One such notable person is Conrad Schumacher. He has already trained students in Germany and Holland to win 37 international medals. Now his quest is to train representatives of other countries to international success. He says, 'I like to teach foreigners. I believe it's better because in Germany we have access to so many good trainers whereas in many countries riders have difficulties with this.' He explains his ideas further, 'The Germans winning all the time suffocates competitiveness. There's no motivation for other countries; this trend must change if we want to keep dressage viable as an Olympic sport.'

He is not a man easily defeated. He says, 'I like to train dressage teams that put sweat on the German foreheads!' He has helped the Dutch achieve many medals

Olympic action

Sven Rothenberger
on Weyden

BELOW
Ellen Brontje on
Petit Prince

Ellen Brontje on Olympic Larius

and his most recent challenge is to uplift Britain into medal status; already individuals have been making breakthroughs in international competitions. A quote from *British Dressage* says:

Jane Bredin on Cupido

> Currently placed 5th in the World Cup standings, Richard Davison and Hiscox Askari demonstrated top form in Paris Bercy (CDI-W) where they achieved unique results for Britain. Richard tied fourth place with Anky Van Grunsven and just one place behind current leader in the World Cup standings, Isabell Werth and Nissan Giorgio who took 3rd place. Richard went on to achieve a remarkable score of 72.16% in the Grand Prix Kür.

In the final at Dortmund Richard secured 7th place and in the Kür achieved 70.83%.

Jane Bredin is one of the riders on the British Team Training programme. She says, 'Conrad is very understanding of how to get the best out of horse and rider and is honest and fair-minded. He teaches everybody with the same intent and genuineness. He works really hard to help us. He's not just coming over to Britain every ten days and going through the motions of teaching the British Team, he really wants us to win.'

Living near the international city of Frankfurt helped Conrad to learn the importance of international differences in training both people and horses. He says:'I've always had contact with Americans and other nationalities and so I learnt early in life that a riding system depends on the breed. For example, if you train a Thoroughbred you can't use the German system, it just wouldn't work. Different countries tend to train different breeds of horses and so different riding systems have evolved. As an international trainer you have to be flexible depending on where in the world you're teaching. You can't always ask the horse to follow German training methods, you can ask for as much as the horse is capable, but keep that flexibility in mind. You have to be flexible to the person you're teaching; all the combinations are so different.'

Another guardian of dressage is Sylvia Loch – to her the horse is the *usce beatha*, the liquid gold water of life. Her aims are twofold: to foster caring attitudes towards horses and to preserve the Classical principles of riding. She says 'You can always tell a trainer who has a deep love of horses. The most obvious facet will be their concern for the horse in the way they teach the rider. This will be the trainer who looks into the horse's eye, who touches his neck, who moves in close to the horse and gives confidence to the whole combination. This is the trainer who watches every move the horse makes and helps him with their own body language. Such a person will always find a reason why the horse could not do something and look to the rider to bring about change, not blame the horse.

'For those of us who love the horse – and it is my belief that there are far more people who seriously respect and want the best for their animals than those who don't – it is important now to find the courage to change attitudes before we return to the dark times . . . It is all too easy to rob a horse of his allure, presence and beauty, to enslave him and to produce a tick-tock machine, a dull robot which bears little relation to the magical creature of speed, grace and light with which we have been blessed.'

Despite all the fluxes and differences, one aspect of dressage is unquestionable – dressage is about progression and learning; the alpha and omega of all equestrianism. We have a responsibility, we must be like passionate vigilantes and guard the horses, both for sports dressage and high school dressage. We must protect the greatness of true dressage and see it grow through this century, and beyond . . .

CHAPTER 2

Mirrors of Classical Dressage

Herr Franz Rochowansky is affectionately known as 'Rocky' in England and 'Rock' in America and is noted as being one of the most talented trainers of the twentieth century.

All who come to know him are astounded by his clarity of thought and the precision of his 'eagle' eyes. He misses nothing – no detail is too small, no amount of time or dedication too much – for Rocky dressage must be right. The ethos of the Spanish Riding School of Vienna lives loyally in his heart, even at his grand octogenarian age.

Rocky has two photographs. One is of his teacher, Polak and the other is of himself, but if you placed them side by side you could believe that one photograph had been duplicated. 'It is how they train at the Spanish School The Master teaches the pupil and it is the pupil's aim to mirror his Master. This could only happen in the School. There is nowhere else like it. It is a way of teaching. The pupil studies hard and long to follow faithfully the traditions of the School, and it is this absolute exactness to its traditions that keeps its teachings untouched, original and fresh.'

Rocky's teacher, Master Polak

Rocky is acclaimed a Master of the piaffe and passage. His dedication to the Classical ideals is legendary – the rider's position, the correctness of the horse's way of going. He was one of the youngest Chief Riders of the Spanish School and held that position for twenty-three years; he was very much involved with saving the Lipizzaner stallions during the Second World War.

A genius with the long reins, he has received the gold Rider's Medal from Germany. This is an award rarely given and only to those of the highest levels of equestrian excellence.

Born a baker's son, Rocky entered the Austrian cavalry and after six years service he was assigned to the Spanish Riding School for eighteen months training. The spur for Rocky's talent lies in his unending passion for horses. His astuteness and great attention to detail are facets that have moulded his success. Historically, being a Chief Rider of the Spanish School elevates the rider to a sort of royalty status – a King of Horsemanship. Rocky lives in the history books of dressage. He believes all knowledge comes from the teacher.

The following extract from *Dressage Today* gives an insight to the School's influence upon Rocky. He talks about his early days at the School and the enthusiasm each student needed to put into learning:

'There were volumes of information to be learned. The student was expected to answer every question 100 per cent correctly. The subject ranged from history to different types of bits and their uses. Those types of questions had only one answer, but queries about the aids for riding called for more elaborate and expansive explanations. Students were expected to demonstrate thorough knowledge of different schools of thought both current and historical.'

A meticulous student always hungry for the next lesson, Rock recorded all he learned about horses in a notebook which he holds dear to this day. To illustrate how well he knows these notes, he says about any training detail, 'Even if you wake me in the middle of the night, I'll give you the same answer.' Although he's read all the notable books on dressage, it is his training at the Spanish Riding School which forms his lessons.

There is no quibbling with Rock. There is only one way to do things, the correct way. If you were to distil Rock's mission in life, it has been to bring to riders the system for riding as he learned it at the Spanish Riding School. He says 'I must teach what I was taught.'

The Olympic rider Vicki Thompson, who has been his student for sixteen years, talks about some of Rocky's ideals: 'The whole idea behind the Spanish

Riding School is to work in empathy with the horse. There are no judges, only trainers. The horses are selected because they are entirely suited to Haute Ecole.

There is a tendency for modern riders to own one or two horses and to want to do dressage, but the fact that a horse may find dressage immeasurably difficult does not seem to be an issue! They become obsessed - they want to teach the horse so much that they sometimes even hit him to make him perform, despite the fact that he is totally unsuited to the job and in the end there is no horse left.

'The Spanish School selects a horse that has the talent for the job required. All horses undergo the basic training, but they are not expected to specialise and excel in everything. For example, one horse may be talented at in-hand work, another at the airs above the ground – whatever they find easiest is the task they are trained to perform.

'In Grand Prix competition work, the horse has to be good at everything – from the highest collected movements such as the pirouettes and piaffe to the extended work in trot and canter. Normally, you find a horse has an aptitude for either extension or collection, but to find one that excels in both is very difficult. This is the big question for the modern competitor.'

Rocky talks with respect about the direction competition riding is taking. 'There has been little change in the direction from the FEI since after World War One until recently, but now Mr Eric Lette is chairman of the FEI dressage committee we are seeing changes.' (Eric Lette was trained by the Swedish Cavalry and rode for a year at the Spanish Riding School.)

Rocky has his own ideas on how he would like to see competition progressing: 'The Grand Prix horses should be tested in an Elementary test which is judged on simple exercises; the impulsion, the straightness, the correctness of figure riding. As in ice skating, this test could be run as a separate show, and then afterwards, provided the horses achieve an acceptable level of competence, they would be allowed to go forwards and be tested in an FEI Grand Prix test. Combining these two elements would improve the way of going of all the top horses, and ensure that the basic training is correct.'

Contrary to what many people believe, Spanish School riders do compete, for example Alois Podhajsky won a bronze medal at the 1936 Olympics; General von Gratz took his Grand Prix horse to Berlin and came 7th. Rocky also competed on Dutch horses when he lived and trained in Holland in the 1960s. However, Rocky says, 'Within the School the riders train the horses. They concentrate on that, no outside influences are allowed to shadow the purity of training and only when the stallions are ready does the School show them in displays and performances in Vienna and on tours around the world.'

Rocky is recognised as one of the foremost dressage trainers since World War Two, particularly in Holland, the USA and Britain. Today, he has handed down his knowledge to international trainer and rider Vicki Thompson. They are based in the southeast of England. No undue pressure is put on the horses because they are taught a discipline they can relate to and understand. Vicki talks about her and Rocky's ways of training: 'We love the horses. We don't want to face them head on and force them into impossible tasks. Often a horse resists because he finds it impossible to understand a rider's request, but if you treat them like children and give them the discipline but be understanding, the horse will say "Nobody explained that in a simple way before, but now I understand I'll do what you want". The trainer must always remember that every horse is a little different. Each horse must be given the right approach to his training, for example the right groom and the right attitude from all the people he meets. Then, with his talents fully primed, he has a real chance of achieving success.'

Vicki mirrors the talents of Rocky, but she possesses her own brand of dressage. She has polished this knowledge to become an international competitor of formidable force. She has represented Britain internationally for many years on many different horses. Today, she concentrates on helping some of Britain's up-and-coming dressage combinations. Besides teaching from her home stables she travels to other parts of the United Kingdom and also abroad, particularly to the USA. She has taught riders and their horses from Novice to Grand Prix.

Some of Vicki's experience comes from working and training with top European trainers. She explains her views: 'A while ago Rocky suggested I seek help from other experts besides himself. For example, I've been helped by Georg Wahl and for competition riding by the Dutch trainer, Bert Rutten. Bert is able to provide expert interpretation from the ground because of his background of knowledge.' (He has schooled many horses to Grand Prix.) All these facets add up to make him exceptional at training competition dressage.'

Vicki gives her thoughts on being trained: 'I believe all riders at every level of dressage benefit from expert tuition from the ground – there is only so much the rider can feel and see whilst sitting on top of the horse. And because, in dressage, through quality comes quality and less equals more, it is of primary importance to get things right from the outset.

'There are so many grey areas in training a horse. For example, the "feel" each horse gives you, and also riding collection and extension; riding the piaffe and the canter pirouettes. Because of the intricacies of the work, it is always better to train under the guidance of an experienced trainer, so that potential grey areas become crisp and clear in the mind of the horse. Otherwise, before you know it, resistances rather than improvements are instilled in the horse - whereas, if the rider had been intelligent and sought help, these misunderstandings would never have occurred in the first place.

'Training must follow consistency, both in terms of how and when the horse is trained and how the aids are applied. However, if the balance of the horse changes for a moment, and this can often happen with a young horse, the rider will have to adapt the aids accordingly, and being so adaptable so quickly can be very demanding on even the best of riders. This is why the Spanish Riding School is so aware of cause and effect. A rider should be instantly aware of an effect and what has caused it and, if the effect is negative, know instantly how to correct it. The ability to ride in this proactive way is the basis of what training is about: it is rewarded to the rider after long and patient training. The quality of this training can only be good if it is established under the guidance of a good trainer. Nothing can replace the one-to-one basis of the trainer teaching the student. This is the fundamental truth of the Classical way of riding.'

LESSON ONE · Training with Vicki Thompson

'Dressage progression is the result of the gradual build-up of correct training. There is no substitute for time if you want to achieve the right results. The continuation and consistency of the basic work, the rebrushing and retouching of the simple exercises, all these factors add muscle power and empathy between horse and rider.'

POSITION OF THE RIDER

'The establishment of a sound, solid dressage position is the base which makes all good dressage possible. The Classical position has originated to enhance the balance of the horse, not to disrupt that balance or to make it more difficult for the horse to respond easily and willingly to the questions asked by the rider.

'The rider's position acts as a stabilising factor to all the language of communication between horse and rider, i.e. the application of the aids. Imagine a fantasy scenario: for ten years a horse talks English with his rider, but overnight the rider stops speaking English and talks in Chinese. How can the horse possibly understand now? He's never spoken Chinese! It may sound ridiculous but this explains why it's so important to apply the aids in a clear and consistent way. This is only achievable if the rider has an independent seat, a seat that breathes

'The rider's position acts as a stabilising factor to all the language of communication between horse and rider' –
Vicki Thompson teaching

life into dressage. We are talking about the ABC of riding; the communication cords of riding.

'A rider who is not able to maintain a correct and relaxed position must have lunge lessons. This is much better than hammering on riding in an unbalanced way, because this will undoubtedly cause the horse to resist against "miscommunicated" aids. A rider who is unable to stay in balance with the horse, or unable to arrange lunge lessons should ride in walk and rising trot only, and then only in easy exercises such as the transitions. Unbalanced riders inflict negative effects on their horses. The rider must be committed to establishing a good dressage position before "proper" dressage riding begins.'

The following are Vicki's tips for establishing good seat and posture.

General Guidelines to a Good Position

1. At all times, the rider's shoulders and hips remain parallel to the horse's shoulders so that the rider sits centrally over the horse's spine.

2. The upper body is held upright, neither tense nor slack but in a relaxed manner. In most circumstances, the upper body sits as close as possible to the horse's centre of gravity.

3. The rider should sit lightly ('carry their own weight') and not lump onto the horse's back like a sack of potatoes.

4. An independent seat means just that: there should be no 'propping up' of the rider's balance either by holding onto the reins or by gripping onto the horse's sides with the legs.

5. The rider must be consciously aware of how to apply the correct aids for whatever the horse is being asked to perform. The rider must always translate these aids to the needs of the horse; for example, the aids for a novice often differ from those for a Grand Prix horse. With a young horse the aids must always be very clear – black and white – but as the horse becomes developed they become lighter and more subtle.

The Seat

1. Sit with supple hips. The hips and seat must have 'resonance' – life – and be in harmony with the horse's movement.

2. To repeat this important point, sit evenly over the horse's spine with your upper body relaxed, upright and balanced.

3. The seat to the knee remains in close contact to the horse, but never gripping or tense.

4. Correct use of the back muscles allows the rider to lighten or brace the back and so alter the effects of the seat, either to allow the energy produced to go more forwards or to keep the energy contained, as in collection.

5. For some aids the rider must be able to apply more weight independently on one seatbone than the other. This is normally done by placing slightly more weight onto the corresponding stirrup bar.

6. The rider thinks of the seat as an extension of the legs.

The Legs

1. The entire length of the rider's legs lie in a downward contact to the horse's sides, but they lie *with life and sensitivity*. 'Inexperienced riders tend to push their legs down forcefully in an effort to achieve this "contact", but this only makes matters worse. The heels are then pushed down too hard, the feet get jammed below the horizontal by this pressure, and this makes the calf muscles both stiffen and become too stretched. Often this has the effect of making the lower legs swing forwards, and the leg aids become hard and insensitive. In dressage, less is more, but more controlled.'

2. The leg aids enlighten the novice horse to the weight aids so that, after training, he learns to interpret the hip aids without the use of the leg aids. The hip aids evolve until they become 90 per cent of the riding aids. The rider can now use the legs in a more complex language to communicate with the horse, for example to ask for a flying change. The more developed the training of the horse, the more the legs play a secondary role to the hips – this is another fundamental reason why a good dressage position is crucial to the success of a dressage rider.

3. If the horse doesn't react to a leg aid, the best policy is to give a stronger aid, and if the horse still doesn't listen give him a tap with the whip. Then start the process again - a light aid, and if he still does not respond, a stronger aid, and if he still does not react, a tap with the whip. Soon you will find the horse learns to pay attention to the lightest of leg aids.

4. Whenever the lower leg needs to be positioned behind the girth only place it one or two inches back, otherwise the leg aids are diminished and the rider's balance tends to tip forward too much. A good example of this is the canter strike-off: in a right canter strike-off the outside (left) leg is positioned very slightly behind the girth. If it is positioned too far behind the girth the left seatbone will lighten and weaken the seat and the effect of this is to throw the rider's balance too much to the right. Also, the left toe will come too close to the horse's side and the left heel will stick out in an ungainly way! The rider will have made double the effort for a quarter of the effect.

5. The seatbone is controlled through the leg and, to be effective, the leg should hang below the hip.

The Shoulders, Arms and Hands

1. The shoulders stay relaxed. The elbows hang in a natural and relaxed way at an angle of 45 degrees to the saddle.

2. The hand closes smoothly around the rein. The reins are held where a ring is worn. When a 'closed' hand is needed, the fingers close smoothly (as if you were wringing water out of a sponge). If the horse does not react to this light squeezing, relax and soften the elbows, allowing the contact to lighten towards the horse's mouth. Then repeat the light squeezing aid.

3. Depending on the needs of the horse, the forearm can soften forwards from half an inch to approximately ten inches.

4. The amount of tension in the forearm is similar to that used when writing with a pen. Sometimes you may have to increase the pressure to give a firmer aid or correction, however you must always aim to get back to a really elastic feeling.

5. Normally, that is unless an indirect or open rein is being used, the thumbs are positioned on top of the rein and the knuckles are slightly angled so that you can just see each little finger.

6. To stabilise one side of the horse, and when you use an indirect rein, the hand is positioned so that the rein lies close to the horse's neck by his withers.

7. For turns and circles use an open rein. This allows the horse's inside foreleg and inside shoulder to move in balance and prevents him from dropping onto his shoulder. For a novice horse the open rein may mean moving the hand one to two inches to the inside, away from the horse's neck. For a more experienced horse it means turning the forearm slightly away from the withers in a similar way to turning a key anti-clockwise in a lock.

LUNGE LESSONS

The first steps of lungeing prioritise the position of the rider. The trainer is looking to see that the rider sits upright and that the seat, legs and hands are correctly positioned and the aids are correctly applied and co-ordinated. Vicki explains, 'The first aim of dressage riding is to develop the horse from the rider's seat, rein and leg.'

For the Novice Rider

'Address the cause and then correct it – this enlightens the rider to the right dressage feelings. The trainer does this by letting the rider know when the riding has created the right result, and also when it has caused an incorrect effect. The rider gradually interlinks this information with the associated feelings of what produces good results and what does not and so the rider's position improves. Work on the lunge is excellent for building rider confidence because it is reasonably safe provided the horse is quiet, sensitive to the aids and attentive. These factors allow the rider to make quick progress in developing an independent seat. A fitted jacket rather than loose, baggy clothing should be worn, because the latter can make it difficult for the trainer to see exactly how the rider is sitting.

'Most novice riders hold on either with the reins or the legs – mostly with the legs, which doesn't allow them to sit in a supple way and down in the saddle. If the balance of the rider is precarious it is better to stick to foundation exercises. An exercise programme can be built to suit the needs of each individual.

'Novice riders must aim to ride from their seats and have independent balance. The most effective way to do this is to be lunged without using the reins whilst riding different exercises. The rider has to learn not to rely upon the reins. This is the first stage of lunge work. However, even advanced riders will start their lunge lessons by going through the same preliminary exercises because it is the best way to check the security of their dressage seats.

Horse ready for lungeing

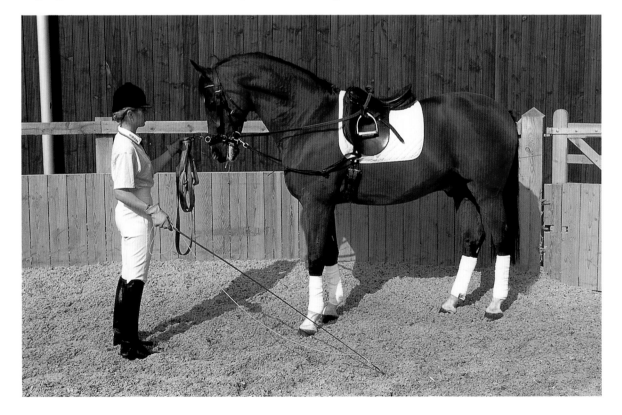

'Simple preliminary exercises give the trainer time to assess the ability, position and balance of the rider. The exercises can then be tailored to suit the needs of each individual. The trainer should always be looking for ways to help improve the rider's balance.

'At the start of a lunge lesson, and as a safety precaution, the horse is loosened-up without the rider. Once mounted, the student should then be given time to become familiar with the horse's rhythm by riding in rising trot.

'A useful way to assess the rider is to ask for half a circle in rising trot and the other half in sitting trot. The trainer should watch how the horse moves under the weight of the rider, especially when the rider makes the change from rising to sitting trot. If the rider is "going with the movement" with supple and relaxed hips the rhythm of the trot stays constant.

'In the sitting trot the trainer is looking to check that the rider's weight comes down correctly onto the seatbones and that the rider sits in a supple and relaxed way. If the rider is stiff and clutches on tightly with the legs, the trainer will see how the horse reacts. For example, the rhythm may slow down, or the horse may move stiffly or be tense.

As a safety precaution, the horse is loosened-up without the rider

'The rider's hands must keep a constant connection with the horse's mouth. They should not suddenly clutch into the stomach, or jump up and down, or shoot up in the air. Such things indicate lack of balance arising, perhaps, from the rider seeking balance from the reins instead of being balanced from the seat. Simple exercises tell the trainer reams about the competence of the student.

'Each individual learns at a different rate. Some people need lots of repetition and corrections before they advance, but the trainer must be patient and understand that this does not mean their ability is less, but just that they learn slowly. No student should be pushed beyond their physical and learning capabilities. This is especially so on the lunge, because lunge lessons can be very demanding physically and mentally. Ideally, the student should be prepared for the more difficult exercises in a gradual "build-up" way, so that when they come off the lunge they are easily within reach of their abilities.'

Vicki is teaching a novice rider on the lunge. The horse has been specifically chosen to benefit the conformation and character of the rider. Vicki asks her to tie the reins in a knot and take rising trot. Once Vicki feels the student is secure enough in her position and is going with the movement of the horse, she brings the horse to halt and asks the rider to take her stirrups away. They continue in sitting trot.

A useful exercise is:

1. The rider lifts both her arms up and out to each side of her body so that they lie level with her shoulders.

2. With the arms held like this the rider turns around so that she faces the trainer in the middle of the circle.

3. She then turns so that she is facing the horse's shoulders again.

4. Next, she turns so that she is facing away from the trainer.

5. Finally she turns around so that her shoulders and hips are parallel to the horse's shoulders and she is sitting in the correct riding position.

The exercise can be repeated several times. The trainer checks to see that:

– The rider's seat stays relaxed, stable and quiet in the saddle.

– She turns from her waist.

– She stretches her torso up from the waist so that the whole of the upper body appears taller.

– During the entire exercise the rider stays in balance with the horse.

In the downward transitions from trot to walk Vicki says, 'Close your leg and ask the horse to return to walk.' In the trot she advises, 'Don't let those ankles and heels jiggle up and down because your lower leg then swings forward and back as the horse moves forwards. Keep your lower leg steady and your upper leg relaxed and supple. Allow the weight to come down through the front of your legs through the knee to supple ankles, and the weight down through the leathers and stirrups onto the balls of the feet. Try to get a steady pressure on the stirrup irons down through the leathers. This will help you to balance your seat.

'To stay sitting correctly let your weight come down through your spine to your seat. Make sure you are sitting for the circle so that you stay sitting centrally over the horse's spine. To do this your outside shoulder and hip will need to come forwards a little and your inside shoulder and hip go back a little.

Exercises on the lunge

'Keep your hands steady. The fingertips must be flat and straight and the thumb on top of the rein. The elbows must stay relaxed. Feel it through your shoulders to your elbows, through the wrists to the horse's mouth. All the time you are riding in that constant rhythm and the pressure on the reins must stay consistent – the weight like a bag of sweets at the end of the reins.

'The upper arms are relaxed and held by your sides, but not glued there! Keep your upper arms soft and the muscles through the elbows and forearm soft. Keep your fists smooth and closed around the reins, but not fixed.'

Lunge lessons last for approximately forty minutes. The rider is progressed to a new exercise only when she has mastered the previous one. She must understand how she is applying the aids – when and in what order – then she learns to ride the exercises and keep her position correct. If the student does not understand fully anything, the trainer explains it until she does, and so the rider associates the right aids with the right effects and consequently gets the right results.

'The trainer only gives corrections when they are needed. For example, if the rider is familiar with an exercise and performs it well the trainer will let the rider know this is good by saying, "Good, that's better". But if it's not correct the trainer will give instructions to make it better and persevere with the exercise until it is done correctly. Sometimes this may mean a rider staying at the preliminary stage for some while, but it is better for the student's riding that the basics are absolutely clear because no real progress can ever be made without them. This early stage of riding establishes the correct dressage position and can take time – sometimes as much as a year or more. I have some students who have taken over two years at the preliminary stage, but once they progress to the more advanced riding they overtake many riders because their basic way of riding is so secure and established. I'm always very proud of them for their perseverance and because they have become good riders.'

For the Advanced Rider

'Bad habits can slip into the riding of even the very best riders and this rubs away some of the harmony between rider and horse. I believe that established riders should have lunge lessons because not only do they consolidate their positions, they also prevent sloppy habits becoming imbedded. For the aspiring rider of advanced dressage, they can really assist in capturing those first feelings of movements such as travers and piaffe. This is because when the horse is being lunged it is easier for the rider to focus on these new feelings rather than on riding the movements. The direction and control of the horse is taken over by the trainer and the rider can relax and "go with" the movements.

'For the more developed rider, the trainer stimulates improvements by keeping the corrections coming thick and fast. For example, the rider could be asked for collected trot and canter through use of the seat and without the reins, and then the same exercise with the reins, followed by single flying changes, travers on the circle, shoulder-in on the circle, the canter pirouettes and the first stages of piaffe. For this type of lunge lesson the rider will need a good degree of fitness.

'When lungeing a student on an advanced horse, I start with simple exercises such as those used for the novice rider. However, the student is quickly progressed to more difficult work, for example collecting the canter and trot through transitions and these exercises are done without using the reins. The rider has to change from the trot rhythm with her hips to the canter rhythm with a more firmly applied inside seatbone so that the horse steps more actively through with his inside hind leg.'

A more difficult exercise than riding without stirrups is riding without the reins, but holding the hands as if you were holding the reins. This is suitable for

Medium strides

Vicki Thompson teaches movements on the lunge – for example, piaffe

ABOVE AND OPPOSITE PAGE: Flying changes are also taught

both the novice and advanced rider. When the student is riding exercises like this, Vicki is looking to see that the student's hips stay supple and 'springy'.

Vicki asks the rider to take the reins and begins other exercises. 'For the downward transition from canter to walk look for the outside rein, make sure your outside leg is feeling and sensitive and do not collapse at the hip. Sit a little firmer and straighter. Let the horse feel the weight aids and he will come in better balance.

'In the half-halt prepare the horse as if you were going to make a stop transition: close your legs a bit so he moves nicely and actively forwards; he is engaged and carrying more weight "up" on his shoulders. He should be obedient and listening to your seat. Keep your hands still. Use your legs, just your legs; sit tall carrying your upper body, close your fists. Have your ankles underneath you so that they hang down beneath your hips. In collection, the rider brings the legs back just a fraction.

'In the upward transitions tread down on the stirrups so that your weight comes more into your seat and then the horse should find a path and go more forwards.'

In the collected canter Vicki says: 'Have the horse a little more round and through from your leg to your hand and more in balance. Have the canter from your seat, not allowing the inside hip to roll forward and not letting your position forward; hold the horse on your seat and allow him to have the freedom to canter. A less refined aid would be, inside leg down so that the inside seatbone presses forward and down, inside hip down, a steady contact with the outside rein. When the horse is cantering on the circle move your inside hand to the inside so you get a good tension on the inside rein. In the canter keep your hands still and your seat steady so you do not disrupt the collected canter rhythm.'

Vicki is particular about how the rider asks for collected canter. 'The rider should sit with the weight more down in the saddle, sitting in a more "up and down" way, but when she pushes too much with her hips from the back to the front of the saddle she rides the horse out of collected canter. For the collected canter the rider sits down a little firmer in the saddle so that when the horse picks his legs up he cannot bring them through so much and take longer strides. He has to get "active" so he is not moving forwards with long strides. Pushing with the seat will flatten the strides. Hold him in your seat and try to relax at the "top" of the canter rhythm. Lighten the hands a little when you have enough collection. The top of the canter is its third beat.

'In the transition from canter to walk sit still, close the reins so the horse comes up to your hands – and close your legs, keep the hips still.

'In the counter-canter ask the horse for a little more position, that is more bend to the outside of the circle. The outside leg and seatbone act as the inside leg and inside seatbone, and the inside leg acts as the outside leg and is positioned a little behind the girth.

'In the medium strides the rider releases the collected energy. To be good, the horse has really got to be listening and reacting to the aids. Of course, the horse must practise this, and also the rider. Sometimes the trainer can help the situation by lungeing the horse and half-halting him so that he becomes more collected and then encouraging him more forwards into the medium steps. The collection improves the engagement and consequently the medium strides.

'The trainer helps the rider to make improvements in position and the "feels" of riding by tailoring the exercises to suit the student's stage of learning. Through correct repetition, the student learns to maintain a correct dressage position in all situations. Lunge riding is a test of physical and mental self-discipline. It builds a framework of riding abilities from which all balanced dressage riding stems.'

DIRECT TRANSITIONS, HALF-TRANSITIONS AND HALF-HALTS

Direct Transitions

Direct transitions and half-transitions are dissected versions of half-halts. They strengthen the horse's back and hindquarters and teach him to be obedient to the rein, seat and leg aids. Simply put, they explain engagement in logical and easy-to-understand terms. For example, the horse learns to understand that the leg aids can mean step through more in the downward transition rather than go forwards more actively.

Vicki explains how to start training them. 'Begin teaching the horse to perform good transitions by riding them in the working gaits. The horse should respond upon command, with ease and at short notice. You will know if the horse is responding well if he makes a transition after you have straightened your back and closed your legs and hands. Initially, the transition can be progressive, but this progression means taking the time to reapply the aids if the horse doesn't understand. If you teach the horse this way he quickly learns to be obedient to the transition aids. For example, as soon as you sit up straight the horse anticipates slowing down and becomes more responsive to the aids. The horse thinks he's being smart, but in reality he's responding to your commands!

'To apply transition aids very precisely, sit straighter and stiller for a moment-but not for too long because the horse will stiffen - and put the legs steadily around the horse's sides. You should feel the horse move more forwards and that more contact has come into the reins. In effect the energy produced has travelled into the bridle because your hands are closed and you have not allowed the forward momentum to be released. The horse will react by engaging himself more and will step more actively and in an engaged way into the downward transition.

'The energy falls onto the hand if the horse pushes into the bridle too strongly. He cannot engage and usually reacts by leaning on the rider's hands. To balance him, release the rein pressure and then close the hand again. In other words, repeat the aids.'

The transition aids must always be applied in the right way – as is the case with all the aids in every situation. 'For example, if you pull on the reins you will shorten the horse's neck. Sit correctly, that is without leaning back, or tipping forwards or collapsing your hips. Learn to feel and be disciplined about your seat, leg and hand aids.

'Transitions gymnasticise the hindquarters and through them the horse stays "up" and forwards. He remains in balance. The degree of carriage he offers does not deteriorate. If the rider asks for these exercises correctly the training is very beneficial to the horse both in the short and long term.'

Half-Transitions

'These are working exercises for the half-halts. Like the direct transitions, they gymnasticise the quarters, but even more so because anything performed slowly is more demanding. In Classical terms, whenever you sit up straight and close your hands and legs you are asking for a half-halt, which is a tension aid. The half-transitions dissect this tension aid so that the horse learns to react in a good style.

'Riding the half-transitions is a discipline of your seat. You proceed as if you were asking the horse to change to a slower gait, for example trot to walk, but just before the horse makes the downward transition his trot become shorter, and at that moment, you urge him forwards again into an active trot. Let the half-transitions be progressive initially: that is, the horse takes time to flow into the downward part of the half-transition and allow more time for the horse to step forwards in the upward part of the half-transition. If you do this he is less likely to make mistakes. You may find that the novice horse can perform the half-transitions more easily on a straight line than on a circle. Give him every opportunity to oblige you.'

Half-Halts

'The half-halts are more polished versions of the half-transitions and are effective when the horse progresses in his training. However, before this stage is reached the horse tends not to react to them in the right way. For example, if the rider puts too much backward pressure on the rein, or the seat and leg aids are not well co-ordinated, the half-halt can become destructive rather than constructive. Initially, the half-halt is used as an attention aid. Teaching the horse to respond well to half-halts is a major part of producing a dressage horse. For example, they can improve the trot tremendously. The rider can "pick up" the forehand, add elevation, suspension and balance to the gait. With the advanced horse the half-halt is still an attention aid but much more refined, more glossy, and much more effective in improving the gaits.

'To produce these good results the horse must be obedient to the rider's seat. The rider should have "resonance", or "life" in the seat that encourages better rhythm. It is all very supple and easy, never brittle.'

FIGURE RIDING

Vicki says, 'Dressage riders must think geometrically. You must be very strict about this. Very precise; very geometric. You ride to the geometry of a correctly proportioned dressage arena so you have a yardstick to measure success because without this yardstick it's impossible to evaluate whether the horse is progressing along the right lines in his training. If they are well ridden, corners, turns and circles automatically balance and engage the horse and this improves straightness and "throughness" of the horse's energy from his hindquarters to his poll. The boundaries of the arena help the inexperienced horse by acting as a guideline that he knows he cannot move beyond. For example, in shoulder-in the track helps to hold the horse's quarters and prevents the shoulder from falling out and in the travers the track helps keep his head and shoulders along a straight line. You could compare the concept to how a child learns to write: first on lined paper so that the writing runs on a straight line, and next on unlined paper, but only when the child has grasped how to keeping the words running in a straight line across the page from left to right.

'The dressage rider develops an "eye" for what is geometrically correct by practising figure riding. For example, a rider who is self-disciplined to always ride properly proportioned circles (20m, 15m, 10m, 8m, 6m) is able to identify precisely:

— Whether the horse is moving accurately along the line of the circle.

— Whether he lacks straightness.

— If he has any stiffness or evasions.

— If he is 'through' to the bridle.

— Whether the rhythm is regular.

The rider can conclude from the information gathered where the horse's weaknesses lie. This informed position makes the rider better equipped to decide how to correct faults. However, without the use of a dressage arena, making constructive decisions would have been much more difficult.'

Turns and Circles

'The first test of figure riding is turns and circles. They focus on the horse's balance, rhythm and acceptance of the rider's aids. When first training the young horse, ride with less concentration upon accuracy. The time to ride precise geometric figures is when his physical strength and suppleness have developed enough to cope with their demands.

'When you ride a corner, a circle, or a turn, bring your outside shoulder and hip slightly forwards and your inside shoulder and hip slightly back to make sure that you sit parallel to the horse's shoulders; in this way you will not disrupt his balance. Be careful that you *turn* the horse round the turns and circles and that you do not pull backwards with the inside rein and unbalance him. To check you are doing this I suggest, particularly with a young horse, that you soften your inside elbow so that you move it slightly forwards to double-check you are not pulling on the inside rein. At the same time, move the inside rein slightly to the inside for an open rein effect. Don't drop the contact on the outside rein even if it becomes a little more weighted than you would ideally like, however, don't weight it so much that you bend the horse's head to the outside.' (For more information on the open rein see section on Shoulders, Arms, Elbows and Hands). When making a turn, any backward pressure on the inside rein makes the horse gather momentum. He falls onto his inside shoulder, he comes out of balance and his rhythm falters. He tips his head, he bends his neck too much to the inside and his shoulder becomes loaded. He may well move in the opposite direction from what you want because the outside rein is not applied. It can be a whole catalogue of disasters if not ridden well.

'In competitions, the first impression a judge gets is how the horse moves up the centre line and how he makes the first turn at C. If the test says "track right", but the horse moves left before tracking right because the rider has pulled on the inside rein what must the judge conclude? Obviously, that the horse is unbalanced and the weight is too much on the inside shoulder and inside rein! How much better if the horse moves smoothly around the turn and there are no resistances, because this means that the horse has a good degree of balance and this is what dressage is all about.

'In all riding go for quality and apply the correct aids. I cannot repeat this piece of advice too often. The horse learns from consistency and repetition – that means you as a rider applying the aids consistently in the same way for each instruction. If you do not get the right response, it is much more sympathetic and effective to reapply the aids.'

GUIDE TO THE WORKING GAITS

'The working gaits are the foundations of dressage; without them no proper dressage training can begin. They supple and prepare the horse, both physically and mentally, for the demands of collection and extension. They should be consolidated so firmly that the horse automatically steps into them without much interference from the rider. The horse has learnt to move under his "own steam" and the first stages of self-carriage have been taught.

'It is important in all the gaits that the rider's legs remain quietly active and harmonise with the rhythm of each gait. Be careful not to curl the legs tightly against the horse's sides. Let the legs enhance the activity and avoid driving the horse forwards too zealously because this hurries the gait out of rhythm.

'The seat should be balanced and not interfere with the rhythm of the gaits; and not drive or be tense which would push the horse out of the tempo onto the hands. The seat *allows* the gait to stay active and balanced. This activity is created from the leg.'

The working gait for the walk is called the medium walk: 'The horse carries himself in a nice, round outline and his hind feet track into, or a little over, the prints made by the forefeet. The aids for the walk are alternate lower leg aids at the moment the horse lifts up each hind leg. If the horse is lazy in walk, ride him more forward with the leg aids and do not push with the seat. The seat follows the movement and the hands allow it. To steady up a fast walk, ride with a slightly "heavier" seat and close the legs so that you hold the gait. To slow the rhythm sit *very* slightly behind the momentum and close the hand, but do not shorten the rein or in any way shorten the walk. Transitions from walk to halt speckled closely together will steady a real "hurrier".

'In the working trot the horse carries himself in a nice, round outline and tracks up or overtracks. To slow down a fast trot use frequent transitions from trot to walk and if the trot is too slow, keep 'life' in your seat, that is, allow the movement through the horse's back. A lazy horse can often be heavy to the leg and if he does not react to the leg aids on the first application re-apply them with slightly stronger indications, sometimes even turning the toes out so that the heels can give a tiny 'prod' by the girth. However, always make sure that you reposition your feet immediately afterwards and only use these more severe aids when and if strictly necessary. If you still do not get enough reaction, tap the horse behind the girth with the whip. Make it a sharp tap so that the horse understands exactly what you want. In between applications of the leg aids, the legs remain neutral, that is they lie quietly around the horse, never gripping, so the horse feels comfortable and can be more sensitive to each aid. Every time you have to sensitise the horse by a) a light squeeze, b) a stronger squeeze, c) a prod and d) a tap with the whip, *always* return to the original, consistent leg aids you normally use - that is the gentlest leg aids that speak kindly to the horse.

'The same principles apply to the working canter as to the working trot. The canter must be bouncy and jumping forwards with three distinct steps. Move the hip up and down in harmony with the movement and avoid over-pushing with the seat. Transitions encourage engagement and tone down an exuberant canter. Sharpen up a lazy horse by correctly applied leg aids, but do not expose him to driving aids that are too strong because this tends to flatten the canter and put him on the forehand.

'The working gaits can act as a "buffer zone" if problems arise later in the training. For example: if the horse has a problem in the collected canter the rider might revert to the working canter and re-establish his confidence and forwardness. The rider will be aware that the horse feels comfortable in his working "gears" and he can perform them easily and with confidence, and this may well solve the problem in the collection. When the horse returns to collected canter he should come back with refreshed vigour and vitality.

'Progress through the working gaits at a speed that suits the individual horse. As a general rule, and providing the horse is in work on a consistent basis, this time period is normally six months to a year.

'Not all the tempos develop at the same rate. Normally the working trot develops first, then the working canter and lastly the medium walk. Once a working gait is established the rider can begin collecting it. In fact, the introduction to collection will have already started by increasing engagement through direct transitions, half-transitions, half-halts and figure riding.

'There is never a day when the rider says, "Right, today the working gaits stop and tomorrow the collected ones start". Working and collected gaits blend into each other and are perfected as the horse gains muscle strength and understanding. Collection is a gradual process, however the rider is aware that the sooner the gaits are collected the more favours are done to the horse.'

GUIDE TO COLLECTING THE GAITS

'Collection lifts weight off the horse's forehand and more onto his hindquarters and this freeing of the forehand makes the gaits more spectacular and expressive. As previously explained, collection develops from the transition and half-halt work. The horse becomes more responsive to the rider's leg aids. The horse's carriage and engagement improve.

'In the collected walk and trot the hind feet step into, or just behind, the prints made by the forefeet. In the collected canter each bound is more elevated, "rounder" and more "through".

'The rider looks to see how the horse tracks up naturally and uses this as a guide to how he should track up in his working and collected gaits. Each horse has his own working and collected gait peculiar to him, and it would be unnatural and conceited to expect the horse to adhere to the principles laid down by the rigidity of academics. As an approximate measure, if a horse's working trot overtracks, his collected trot would track up, but if the working trot tracks up rather than overtracking then his collected trot would undertrack (that is the hind feet step just short of the hoofprints made by the forefeet). A good rider has an innate feel for what is right for each individual horse and should be guided by this feeling, by accumulated knowledge and by the advice of their trainer.

'In collection the horse must move actively underneath himself and not run too much onto the bridle or get tense, or lazy. Go back to the preceding steps of collection and perfect the half-transitions if the horse exhibits resistances. Make the corrections so that the horse understands the aids exactly and then he will always react readily and with more obedience.

'The *biggest problem with collection* is that the rider hears the word "collection" and starts *to pull the horse's front end backwards*. This *shortens the horse's neck and back, restricts the activity* in the hind legs, *displaces the horse's shoulders* and makes him go *crooked*. At this point, the horse can even become stronger and resistant to the rider's hands. It is essential that the rider sits with "resonance", that is, with life in the hips, and that this resonance is maintained so the rhythm and way of going of the horse are not disrupted.

'Start training the collected trot from the half-transitions, but make sure the horse does not run forwards from your leg aids. He must react with life and energy in his hind legs from a softly applied leg aid. Sit with a balanced and supple position and keep your hands steady so you do not disrupt the rhythm. Most importantly, *the rein aid part of the half-halt must be positive* – to check you follow this principle *allow your hands to move fractionally forwards before you close them.*

'The same rules apply for the collected canter as for the collected trot. Pay attention that you are not over-driving the horse with your seat, because this will push his hind legs too far under his body and unbalance him and you will get increased problems, not better collection! The hind legs will concertina under the horse so much that he cannot contain the collection with his forelegs and so pulls into the bridle (he will either pull downwards or upwards, whichever is his inclination). Ride with a lighter seat, a more up-and-down inclination which allows the horse to work actively underneath you. The seat is used more as a feeling than a direct aid; a lifting up of your ribs and hips.

'In the collected walk the horse must step actively forwards with a nicely carried head and neck. He remains in a consistently good frame and maintains the regularity of the walk steps. Be careful not to disrupt the gait, but encourage the walk forwards.

'The diagnostic signs of tension which tell you if the horse is not yet ready for the demands of collected walk are:

1. If you feel the head carriage is incorrect in any way.

2. The horse comes behind the bridle.

3. The horse is unsteady in his mouth.

'True collection is only possible if the horse moves straight. Collection (if taught correctly) physically improves the horse and this is one of the greatest bonuses handed to us from Classical dressage – treasure this gift.'

GUIDE TO LENGTHENING THE GAITS

Lengthening Steps in Trot

'The right environment for lengthened trot is introduced by the rider increasing the engagement and activity of the horse. He reacts by lengthening his frame so that he steps into the movement and remains in balance. The horse steps with an activated hind leg further under his body than he would do for the working trot. This increased engagement propels his energy forwards and up through his shoulders. This energy becomes translated so that he strides forwards with his forelegs into equal lengthened strides.

'Initially, only ride a few steps of lengthened trot at a time, and then only when the horse is strong enough to maintain a good level of balance and rhythm, because unless he is sufficiently muscled and strengthened in his back and hind legs this work puts weight onto his forehand – which is the opposite of what we want in dressage. Some horses are naturally talented at lengthened and extended trot. Be careful because you can so easily spoil this talent. Allow the correct

Lengthened trot

technique to develop when the horse becomes physically stronger and more developed, otherwise you may find his talent is left unrealised and inconsistent.

'To prepare the horse for the lengthened strides keep your weight down in the saddle and apply your legs so that the horse becomes more active underneath you. Once he is engaged in this way apply the leg aids so that his hind legs become more activated and his forehand lifts: now he will trot into lengthened strides.

'Do not bang your legs against the horse's sides and interrupt his trot strides. Your seat stays passive and follows the movement of the lengthening. Keep your hands steady. More tension may come into the rein as the horse stretches to lengthen: as he stretches, allow the contact to follow in an elastic way. Do not yield the contact before he stretches, because he may drop the connection with the bit and falter onto his forehand, run and hurry. Sit heavier again when you ask for the transition back to working trot and combine this seat aid with applying your legs and closing your hands. Lengthened strides will naturally flower into medium and extended trot when the collected trot, balance and carriage of the horse have been well established.'

Extending the Steps

In the extended gaits the horse steps through to his maximum stride without losing rhythm and balance. The hind legs propel the horse forwards and he stretches his head and neck forwards to lengthen his frame without coming onto the forehand. Vicki explains the most common problems to avoid:

1. Incorrectly preparing the steps preceding the extension. For example, shortening the horse's neck in the collected trot.

2. Not allowing the horse to stretch out enough and upsetting his balance.

3. The horse's face line coming behind the vertical. This tightens his top line.

4. Demanding too much extension at the beginning of the movement so that the horse speeds up and loses his trot rhythm.

'The medium and extended canter are similar to the trot. Make sure that the strides cover "upward and forward" over the ground, rather than the horse dropping his frame and quickening the stride and coming too much on the forehand. The canter should show big, bouncy, free strides. Be careful not to sit down and push too strongly because this could flatten and stiffen the horse's back.

'The extended walk demonstrates correct training. The horse has to maintain the

1, 2, 3, 4 rhythm of the walk and really step forwards actively. Alternate your legs aids to encourage this stepping forwards by applying each alternate aid *in time with the corresponding hind leg*. For example, when the left hind leg is stepping forwards apply the calf muscle of your left leg against the horse's side for the duration that the left side of the horse moves forwards, and as you feel the right hind leg coming forwards keep the left leg passive and then apply the calf muscles of your right leg against the right side of the horse. These alternating lower leg aids help the horse to step forwards more actively. The seat should not drive but move in a supple and relaxed (not slack) way, with the movement of the walk. The rider must maintain a contact with the horse's mouth, and at no time drop the contact so that the movement is downgraded to a free walk on a long rein, which is a different exercise altogether.

'Throughout the extended walk the horse must stay relaxed but active and be allowed the time to complete each step of the walk so that it does not become disrupted. If you develop a good collected walk so the horse walks *actively* with a free and loose step through the shoulder, you will find the horse will walk with more suppleness and this will help improve the quality of the extended walk.'

INTRODUCING LATERAL WORK

'You can start the lateral work when the horse remains balanced through turns and circles. Stay flexible in your attitudes and respond to the needs of each individual horse. For example, the right time to start the lateral work is not necessarily connected to the horse's age. It often varies depending on his developed muscular strength, his balance and the way he moves. We tend to introduce the shoulder-fore fairly early in the training, even if it's just in walk. Be advised that if done incorrectly this work can disrupt everything.

'Gaits always have authority over movements. The only exception to this rule is when you begin explaining the movement to the horse, and then only for a fleeting moment. Dressage should improve the gaits, not ruin them. Most importantly, the rider should remember that lateral work focuses on sideways and forwards and should avoid being obsessed with the "sideways" and forgetting the "forwards"!'

Shoulder-Fore

'Shoulder-fore positions the horse's forehand to the inside of the track by an angle of ten to fifteen degrees. The horse moves so that his inside foreleg is positioned just slightly on a new track to the inside. In shoulder-in (as required in competition) the horse moves at an angle of thirty degrees and thus shoulder-fore is the easier movement, this being the reason why it is usually taught before the shoulder-in. Both movements are ridden in a similar way.

'Training shoulder-fore can begin when the rider can control the horse's shoulders and maintain the correct bend. Once the horse can maintain his balance, rhythm and the correct angle on both reins in walk shoulder-fore, the trot shoulder-fore can be started.' (See table on page 47.)

'Shoulder-fore can be ridden in canter and is particularly beneficial in strengthening the horse's hindquarters and straightening the canter. However, be careful of canter shoulder-fore because, if it is not ridden correctly, it can be very disruptive to the canter. A rider new to lateral work will find canter shoulder-fore difficult and because of its inherent dangers if ridden incorrectly, I would advise canter shoulder-fore being ridden under the instruction of an experienced dressage trainer.'

Shoulder-In

'Normally in competition shoulder-in the horse is positioned at a thirty degree angle to the track. To explain this more fully: the horse's forehand is positioned so that he steps with his outside foreleg on the inside line of the track; and positioned this way the horse looks across in a diagonal line to the opposite side of the arena. If you stand in front of a horse moving in shoulder-in you will see three, not four, of his legs (the outside hind leg, the outside foreleg which hides the inside hind, and the inside foreleg). This is the most common form of shoulder-in practised today.

'The rider teaches shoulder-in once the horse can perform shoulder-fore fluently and well. As previously explained, shoulder-in is similar to shoulder-fore, but is the more advanced movement of the two.

'A rider who can control the horse's shoulders to an exact degree (i.e. from an angle of five degrees up to forty) has the chance to perfect straightness and uses shoulder-in to maximise the horse's engagement, suppleness and acceptance of the bridle. It enables the rider to piece together other exercises, for example the half-pass and pirouette. Keeping the horse's forehand in advance of his hindquarters is fundamental to the physics of forward momentum.

Vicki follows the principles of many top trainers: 'Shoulder-in must be ridden correctly otherwise it becomes disruptive rather than constructive. Absolutely essentially, the horse must be working to the outside rein. In the shoulder-in, as in all the lateral movements, the quality of the steps must remain consistently true in rhythm.

Table 1. **Riding the Shoulder-Fore**

SEAT	The inside seatbone is weighted.
SHOULDERS AND HIPS	Turn the inside shoulder and hip slightly back and the outside shoulder and hip slightly forwards. **Tips** • Always sit parallel to the horse's shoulders.
INSIDE LEG	How you use your inside leg is vital to the success of this movement. Let it hang down naturally so that it is positioned underneath your hip and seatbone. The leg must be active, but not so tight that it holds the horse's forehand on the track so he cannot do a shoulder-fore! **Tips** • If you apply the inside leg too early, before the horse's shoulders are properly positioned, you won't get shoulder-fore but perhaps just too much neck bend. Hold the inside leg soft against the horse's side so he can carry his forehand to the inside of the track.
OUTSIDE LEG	The outside leg is passive. It hangs down naturally by the side of the horse, and if the rider is sitting correctly – that is square to the horse's shoulders – it will automatically hang down an inch or two behind the girth. The outside leg is rarely further back behind the girth. **Tip** • Should the horse rush forwards too quickly, the outside leg can be used to re-establish the correct rhythm, and once this is achieved, it should resume its passive role.
OUTSIDE HAND	The outside hand remains still and keeps a consistent and steady outside contact while at the same time allowing the inside bend. The outside rein is usually held close to the horse's neck. **Tip** • Normally, the horse's neck should never be bent more than the amount of bend he can show through the length of his body.
INSIDE HAND	The inside hand is 'open' and with a young horse this is as much as 3–5cm (1–2in). The hand is held in this open position for the duration of shoulder-fore. (See also Riding The Shoulder-In, page 49.) The rider 'softens' the contact on the inside rein if the horse takes too heavy a hold, but otherwise the hand remains perfectly still. **Tip** • Softening the inside rein and then giving the rein so that the horse is in self-carriage will show he is truly established on 'inside leg to outside rein' and is a good test to check that the rider is not pulling on the inside rein. This 'softening' develops better flexion and gradually, over a period of time, effects a more equal acceptance of the bit in the horse's mouth.

Three-track
shoulder-in

'Use the walk to teach shoulder-in and, when the horse can maintain rhythm and balance in this gait, you can progress to trot shoulder-in. Shoulder-in asks the horse to step under his body with activated hind legs and this gymnasticises them so that he is physically better equipped to lighten and carry his forehand. It plays a major role in dressage by straightening the horse, improving the carrying abilities of his hind legs and preparing for some of the more difficult lateral exercises.

Table 2. **Riding the Shoulder-In**

SEAT	The inside seatbone is weighted. **Tip** • If you are riding the shoulder-in angle accurately your body should be positioned directly above a line on the inside edge of the track.
SHOULDERS AND HIPS	Bring the inside shoulder and hip back a little and the outside shoulder and hip forwards a little so that you are looking across the diagonal line. **Tips** • Ensure you remain sitting centrally over the horse's spine and in balance with the movement.
INSIDE LEG	The horse is bent around the rider's inside leg, which is placed on the girth and applied softly against his side. Once the horse is more responsive to the inside leg it will be enough for the rider to emphasise the inside seatbone aid by treading down slightly more on the inside stirrup. At this stage of training the horse should understand this subtle aid as the inside leg aid. **Tips** • Make sure that your inside leg is not gripping up and too far back from the girth because this moves the horse's haunches to the outside of the track and creates too steep an angle. The horse may find this too difficult and react by pulling himself forwards out of the shoulder-in. Don't stick the inside leg forwards by the horse's elbow because you will interfere with the correct position of the horse's shoulders.
OUTSIDE LEG	Your outside leg is passive. **Tip** • If the horse rushes forwards too quickly apply the outside leg slightly behind the girth, but once good rhythm is resumed the outside leg continues in its passive role. • The outside leg can act as a prompt to the young horse new to shoulder-in and indicates that he must step off the track into the shoulder-in position. But immediately he has done this the outside leg must resume its passive role. (This aid is only used as a short-term measure to make it very clear to the horse exactly what is required.)
INSIDE HAND	The inside rein is passive and open – this means it is positioned in front of your inside hip. **Tip** • Be wary of this aid, if you carry your inside hand towards the horse's wither or backward towards your tummy, you will create too much bend and push the horse's shoulders out – which is exactly the opposite to what you want to achieve!
OUTSIDE HAND	The outside rein carries the most weight and maintains the correct shoulder-in position to the inside of the track. **Tips** • Be careful with your hands. Many times problems with shoulder-in derive from too much bend in the neck alone.

Travers

'Initially, travers is taught as an obedience exercise to the rider's outside leg aids, but later it prepares the horse for the more difficult demands of the half-pass and the canter pirouettes. Travers can be ridden in walk, trot and canter. In travers the horse's quarters move to the inside of the track at an angle of some thirty degrees.

Travers

Table 3. **Riding Travers**

SEAT	The weight is more on the outside seatbone. **Tip** • For three-track travers the outside seatbone will automatically become more weighted if you sit parallel to the horse's shoulders as explained below.
SHOULDERS AND HIPS	Move your outside shoulder and hip back a little and move your inside shoulder and hip slightly forwards. **Tips** • Ensure that you always remain sitting centrally over the horse's spine and in balance with the movement
INSIDE LEG	The inside leg on the girth generates the forward momentum and regulates the amount of inside bend. **Tips** • The inside leg hangs naturally down the side of the horse. Make sure it is not placed too far behind the girth because this pushes the horse's quarters back onto the track; nor that it is positioned too far forwards on the girth, which pushes the horse's shoulders out.
OUTSIDE LEG	The outside leg is positioned behind the girth and used actively to ask for the sideways steps. **Tip** • Make sure you do not bring your outside leg back more than 5cm (2in). This lessens the effect of the outside seatbone and outside leg.
INSIDE HAND	The inside rein is held close to the withers and keeps the bend to the inside. **Tip** • The inside rein can be used in a 'softening' way to make the horse more consistent onto the outside rein and more soft and yielding on this side of his jaw.
OUTSIDE HAND	The outside rein is held a little away from the withers and controls the amount of bend and the outside shoulder. The position of the rider's hand stays consistent. **Tips** • Do not take too strong an outside contact because this will prevent the horse from being able to bend to the inside. The outside contact must be held consistently and steadily but never so tightly that it restricts the inside bend.

'Introduce the travers once the shoulder–in is established, and initially in walk. Ideally, in the travers the horse should be flexed slightly to the inside which means that he will be looking in the direction he is moving. At the early stages of travers, focus on the important parts of the movement: the rhythm, the quality of the gait, the horse's obedience to the outside leg aids, and the travers position along the track; once these are secure ask for a more correct travers with inside bend. Initially, very little bend is expected, but as the horse becomes more supple he will find it easy to maintain balance and more bend can be asked for. The horse can progress to trot travers once his walk travers is fluid and easy. The same rule applies for canter travers, which is begun when the horse is proficient at trot.

'Once the horse has developed an improvement in canter collection, the canter travers exercises can be practised to prepare for the canter pirouette (covered more fully under The Pirouettes, page 54.) In all the work the rider must remain conscious of only introducing the more demanding aspects of a movement when the horse is capable of its easier parts.'

DEVELOPING LATERAL WORK

'In all dressage training empathise with the horse and always be aware of the limits of his strength and ability at any particular time in the training schedule.

Half-Pass

'The half-pass best illustrates the horse's brilliance at forwards and sideways expression. Teach it once shoulder-in and travers are established. To preserve the forwardness make sure that the horse's shoulders are always positioned slightly in advance of his hindquarters.

'Begin teaching half-pass with a few steps in walk. For example, ride a half-circle from the long side of the arena to the centre line and half-pass the horse back to the track. Once the horse understands walk half-pass he can be taught trot half-pass, but to start with do not insist on too much bend or angle. Prioritise on good rhythm, balance and activity.

'If the horse has learnt lateral work in a step-by-step way, this guarantees that he *understands* what the rider is asking and this encourages him to respond positively. Also, the exercises will have helped him gymnastically. But now the time comes to introduce increasingly difficult lateral work. For example, shoulder-in for half of the long side of the track, then a 10m circle, and continue in travers down the track.

'In the more difficult work the rider pays great attention to the correctness of the movements, the exactness of the angles, the precision of the bend, the consistency and activity, the "throughness" of the horse to the bridle and the whole balance of the movements. Now only total accuracy will suffice, but by having followed a steady approach to the training the rider lays the foundations of the horse's ability to cope with the demands of the more advanced movements. For example, the half-pass work advances to half-pass zigzags in trot and canter and culminates in the beautiful, sweeping half-passes shown at Grand Prix level. These express the horse's self-carriage, balance and highly developed levels of good quality collection.'

Table 4. **Riding Half-Pass**

SEAT	If you need more sideways movement and less forwardness, weight the outside seatbone more and half-halt the horse on the outside rein. At the same time use a more active outside leg. If you need less sideways and more forward movement, put more weight onto the inside stirrup and ask the horse more forwards with the inside leg.
SHOULDERS AND HIPS	Be sure you sit centrally over the horse's spine. **Tips** • Don't tip to the outside or collapse your hips away from the movement.
INSIDE LEG	The inside leg asks for extra impulsion and maintains the inside bend.
OUTSIDE LEG	The horse steps sideways by reacting to the pressure of the outside leg positioned behind the girth. **Tip** • To maintain the active strength of the outside leg bring it back to a maximum of 2in. Remember, your seatbone is an extension of your leg and if you bring the leg too far back you weaken the effect of the leg aids.
INSIDE HAND	The inside rein asks for bend and leads the horse into the direction of the half-pass. **Tip** • Do not hold the inside rein too tightly because this restricts the movement of the horse's inside shoulder.
OUTSIDE HAND	The outside rein regulates the amount of bend and is normally used as an indirect rein. **Tips** • The role of the indirect rein in the half-pass, is to encourage the horse to step more sideways. • If the horse shows too much bend to the inside the rider places the outside rein in line with the outside hip and weights it more.

The Pirouettes

'In the pirouettes the horse's forehand moves around his haunches in a turn (180 degrees for a half-pirouette and 360 degrees for a full pirouette). The radius of the circle is equal to the horse's body length. The haunches move so the circle is nearly on the spot, but not quite – that is to say the inside hind leg is picked up and put down in rhythm with the canter. This ensures that the integrity of the gait is maintained. Pirouettes can be performed in walk, canter and piaffe.

'The pirouette is the ultimate canter movement and is very demanding physically on the horse, the inside hind leg bearing the most burden of work. To make the turn the horse has to move his forehand around more quickly than his hindquarters.

'The pirouette is a combination of shoulder-in and travers aids. To explain this more fully:

1. The shoulder-in prepares the horse by straightening the gait and engaging the inside hind leg. It also ensures that the horse's forehand is always slightly in advance of his quarters – this being essential to maintain forward momentum.

2. The travers holds the outside of the horse to the circle. This allows him to make "half-pass" steps sideways with the hind legs so that each step has the same length and energy. When he can do this exercise the rider knows he is ready to learn the canter pirouette - that he is physically capable of turning so that he canters around in a small circle which is almost on the spot.'

Walk Pirouettes

'The rider can start teaching the walk pirouettes once the horse can perform shoulder-in, travers and collected walk. Initially, ask for travers on a large circle, and in the early stages, never ask for travers on too small a circle. The preparatory work for the walk pirouette assists in the training of the collected walk, but if the walk is not collected enough neither the steps nor the circle will ever be small enough to constitute a correct walk pirouette.

To ride a walk pirouette, position the horse in shoulder-fore and lead the forehand forward and sideways to the inside with the inside rein. The outside aids come into play (usually) on the second and third strides. The rider's outside leg stops the horse from following through and stepping out. Do not push the horse in to the inside of the circle too much because then he will cross his hind leg over too much and fall out through his shoulder. Most importantly, make sure the regularity of the walk (before and during the pirouette) is maintained and that the steps are of equal length. As with the canter pirouette, never repeat the exercise again and again.'

Table 5. **Riding Walk Pirouettes**

SEAT	The seat must stay parallel to the horse's shoulders all the time. **Tip** Because you will be preparing the horse to make the pirouette by a combination of shoulder-in and travers aids, the pirouette aids will vary: 1. The preparation for the pirouette aids is normally with the shoulder-in aids. 2. The travers aids hold the outside of the horse onto the turn of the pirouette and keep him disciplined and reactive to the outside leg aids.
SHOULDERS AND HIPS	The rider's shoulders and hips stay parallel to the horse's shoulders – so, of course, they must mirror the horse's forehand as it moves around in the pirouette.
INSIDE LEG	The inside lower leg keeps the engagement of the horse's inside leg and prevents him from throwing his quarters too quickly around the turn. This leg, combined with the outside rein, stops the horse turning in the pirouette and is used to ask him to move out of it and onto a straight line. **Tips** • Horses differ as to how much outside and inside aids they need and these aids can vary even with the same horse depending on whether it is a left or right pirouette. For example, if the horse should be turning more quickly into the pirouette, more outside leg is needed. But if he turns too quickly, less outside leg is needed and more inside leg. More weight on the outside rein holds him to the turn.
OUTSIDE LEG	Positioned approximately 2in behind the girth, the outside leg asks the horse to move sideways and bends him around the rider's inside leg. **Tip** • Be careful that the outside leg doesn't slip too far behind the girth because, as already explained, this reduces the effectiveness of the leg aids.
INSIDE HAND	The inside rein asks for, and maintains the bend. **Tip** • Keep the hands light so that the energy is not restricted.
OUTSIDE HAND	The outside rein is more weighted and stops the horse from bending too much to the inside and loading his inside shoulder. **Tips** • If the shoulders need to be turned more quickly, combined with the use of the outside leg, the outside rein can be used in an indirect way. See Position Of The Rider (page 21) for more details.

Starting the Canter Pirouettes

'The canter pirouette is the "highest" movement for the canter because the horse has to make very small steps with his hind legs but still be active and carry a lot of weight on his quarters. There is a lot of engagement and balance required in the canter pirouettes', Vicki says. 'As already explained, the base exercises are the travers and shoulder-in on the circle. Travers on the circle teaches obedience of the hindquarters to the rider's outside leg aids, and the circle in shoulder-in supples and prepares the horse for the task of turning his shoulders in the pirouette. Both exercises test his concentration and ability to listen to the rider's canter pirouette aids. Because of the demands put on the horse's physique in this exercise you must:

1. Establish collected canter.

2. Consolidate smooth and active transitions into collection and out again – this is essential, because you have got to be able to get in and out of the pirouette easily, and the horse has to be able to make small canter steps at the same time as performing a small turn with his forehand around his quarters.

'Be aware: if the horse falls in and out of a simple turn or circle he is bound to fall in and out of the pirouette and he is obviously not ready for the difficulties of this exercise! When the horse is trained correctly in *all* the preparatory exercises for the canter pirouette, and can remain balanced in the collected canter, you can start riding the canter pirouette.

'Begin by riding across one of the diagonals and, as you approach the spot where you intend to ask for the canter pirouette, start positioning the horse in shoulder-fore. Now start to turn him on the small circle, but in canter travers position. It is preferable in terms of the horse's physical development and understanding of the canter pirouette to keep the circle slightly larger than it ideally should be, and always keep the canter steps regular and the turning of the pirouette smooth. Once the horse can perform a reasonably good canter pirouette, and respond well to the shoulder-in and travers positions, you can begin to demand more exactness in the size of the circle. For a good canter pirouette the circle described by the hind legs should be as small as a dinner plate.

'Because of the demands on the horse in this work and because of the expertise needed to ride it correctly, it is wiser for the less experienced person to ride it only under the guidance of an expert dressage trainer. Practice itself does not make the canter pirouette good, only *good* practice will bring good results.'

An experienced horse showing the degree of engagement needed for canter pirouettes

ADVANCING THE CANTER

Simple Changes

This movement expresses the quality of the collected canter. 'The horse must slow down, shorten himself, engage his hindquarters and carry his forehand to make the good downward transition, and then make good forward-thinking walk steps before the next strike-off into canter. These transitions are quite difficult to do well.'

'In the simple changes the rider is looking for better quality collection and better response to the aids. The horse must be able to "wait" a step or two in the collected canter before we ask him to walk. The biggest problems are that the rider pushes too strongly with the seat and pushes the hind legs too far under the horse's body so that he cannot maintain balance and then it becomes a physical impossibility for the horse to collect. The rider should look for a build-up of balance without too much power. To help the horse achieve good balance the rider sits with independent balance and lightness in the seat.' (See Transitions and Collected Canter sections for more details on how to ride the simple changes.)

Single Flying Changes

'The horse must have developed a good quality canter before he is taught the flying changes. The canter must have a clear period of suspension – this being the moment in the canter when the horse changes his legs in the air and thus makes the flying change. Some horses offer them quite naturally but sometimes they can be detrimental to training if taught too early. So it is safer to improve the quality of the collected canter and increase the level of obedience to counter-canter before teaching the single flying changes.

'The changes motivate the canter so that it becomes bouncier, with more jump. However, if the canter it too "big" and has too much expression the horse will lack control after the change and this could ruin the canter, making it tense and perhaps irregular. The tempo of the canter is vital to the quality of the changes, and if the tempo is in any way erratic you will need to revert to more obedience exercises (simple work such as collected canter and transitions). To maintain a reasonable level of balance after the flying changes the horse must first have sufficient muscular development, strength and suppleness.

'To add potential for the change to be free and to step through to the new lead the rider can give an "attention" aid on the leading rein. This condenses the stride on that side. For example, if cantering right and the flying change will be to the left, half-halt on the right rein because that closes the right side of the horse and he will become more responsive to the leg aids. The inside seatbone lifts up *slightly* and allows a clear passage for the change to step through. Once the horse has performed the change the rider sits deep again, controls the canter strides and keeps the connection (if a "green" horse makes too big a jump, allow it expression and afterwards tone the canter down into better balance.

'As the horse can recover his balance from the single changes more quickly (that is, he can perform a single change and maintain the same rhythm before and after the change), the rider knows he is ready to be taught sequence changes. He accepts, and is comfortable with, doing the single changes and the rider should have no difficulty in linking single changes together. The rider may observe that the strides between each flying change pick up the momentum of the canter so that often the canter improves from this work. For the thinking rider this offers another exercise to create more expression in the canter tempo. The rider can then ask that each flying change is more "up" and forwards-going and more expressive. Through this work the horse automatically increases in strength and becomes more consolidated in his canter balance. A spiral of positive energy is created; this is dressage at its best.'

Table 6. **Riding the Single Flying Changes**

SEAT	The aids are synchronised so that the canter rhythm is the same before and after the change.
HIPS AND SHOULDERS	Sit with the inside hip lighter to allow the change to step through, and with the outside hip down. **Tip** • Be careful you do not twist your body in all directions because this will only unbalance the horse.
LEGS	The leg aids for the canter are reversed: a. What was originally your outside leg slides forwards to the girth. b. What was originally your inside leg slides behind the girth and is applied as the signal for the horse to step through with his outside hind leg and inside foreleg together – this making the change.
HANDS	Keep the hands light so you do not restrict the jump of the canter from moving forwards through into the change. A fraction of a second before the leg aids are applied the rider changes the flexion so that the new inside rein is lighter, and the new outside rein established.

THE FIRST STEPS OF PIAFFE

The piaffe is the ultimate expression of contained energy. 'We call the initial training of piaffe the half-steps. The right time to teach this advanced work is personal to each horse and it depends so very much on the horse's attitude, ability and temperament. For example, with a nervous horse you would need to take a long time to explain the piaffe aids to him quietly. However, an easy-tempered horse can be taught the half-steps earlier in his training.

'In a nutshell, how and when you train the half-steps depends not only on the horse, but on the training methods the rider follows and the talent of the rider to ask for this movement. For example, should the piaffe be progressed in-hand without burdening the horse with the rider's weight? Or should it be developed by riding the horse, but with the assistance of a trainer on the ground? Or should the rider develop it from the very beginning, through riding and without any outside influences? The decision as to which path to follow is decided by the needs of the horse and the system of training with which the rider feels most comfortable.

'The first piaffe steps, that is the half-steps, are shortened, forward-going trot steps which are sometimes produced out of the walk but with other horses from a slow trot. The choice depends on the reactions of each horse. The rider brings the lower legs back a little, and gently and quietly asks the horse forwards from subtle aids. The seat is kept light and the hands are kept light; the horse comes under the rider's weight. Gradually, the horse gains strength and understanding and the half-steps progress into the piaffe.

'For a long time, and until the horse is working well in the half-steps, they are kept inching forwards because this enhances the forwardness: piaffe on the spot is trained only when the horse's strength, forwardness and understanding have become totally established.

'In the piaffe, the horse drives himself more forwards, more "up" than in the vertical way of going of the collected trot, however, he stays in balance a similar way. In the piaffe he picks his hind feet up so that they come directly under his body, his hind hooves coming *just* under his hind legs so that the energy is transferred upwards and the forwardness becomes very elevated.'

VICKI THOMPSON'S TRAINING TIPS

Vicki produces horses who go happily, expressing flair without tension. Below she summarises her priorities in training:

1. The rider must constantly be in 'think-tank' mode, always keeping open the lines of communication with the horse; always understanding that every horse is an individual.

2. The best way to learn is to steep yourself in a learning atmosphere.

3. A well-trained horse gains confidence in himself:
    a. By building up his physical abilities gradually so he can perform the job he is asked to do.

    b. From understanding what he is being asked to do.

    c. From the knowledge of where he stands in the order of his life in terms of routine, consistency and repetition of his training.

    All these factors increase his abilities.

4. Horses from the same bloodlines often exhibit similar behavioural patterns. This knowledge can be a useful resource for the trainer.

5. The ultimate aim of dressage is that the horse stays in balance and harmony with his rider.

6. The horse's balance is derived from self-carriage.

7. A good trainer will always put the horse's needs first and be honest about whether a horse and rider suit each other.

8. Listen to the advice you are given because life is too short to be continually going down blind alleys in a confused muddle.

9. Go to the best trainer you can, and if you cannot afford the very best go to the best that you can afford. It would be better to have fewer lessons from a good trainer than dozens from an inadequate one.

10. Watch as much good dressage as you can.

11. Feed yourself information from every dressage angle.

12. Remember, dressage equals quality not quantity.

13. Steer away from short cuts – they do not exist, except in the minds of impatient riders.

14. At all times the rider must promote mental self-discipline.

15. When training young horses:

    a. Avoid grinding on forever on one point because this can easily sour the horse.

    b. With a novice horse it is not what you do, it is the problems you avoid – in other words, what you do not do. It is much better to stay out of the problem in the first place!

    c. Prioritise putting the aids and communication systems in place.

16. The quality of the gaits takes precedence over everything.

17. Keep your mind open and fresh to logical and humane thoughts.

18. In dressage you never stop learning.

19. Sometimes the rider may hit a 'blockage' in training, but by reverting to simpler work, perhaps consolidating the basic gaits, and/or analysing the problem, the answer appears by itself.

20. Progression springs from a gradual build-up of correct training.

21. As explained at the beginning of this chapter, all riders benefit from expert tuition from the ground because there is only so much the rider can feel, and see, whilst sitting on the horse.

VICKI THOMPSON'S PROFILE

Her elegance rivals the best. A Rembrandt of a rider with an air of mystique and a streak of feminine logic that fascinates most men. There is no brash glamour, just a supremo style of riding.

Life has not always been easy for Vicki Thompson; at nineteen she broke her back in a riding accident. She says, 'A horse bolted with me and I fell off, but you know how it is, when you can't do something you want to do it more and not being able to ride made me even more determined.' It was this persistence that got her back in the saddle six months later.

Lorelie Sea Hifi was her first Grand Prix ride. 'He was such an armchair of a horse. My mother bought him for me when I was in Young Riders; a bright bay with four white socks. He was such a polite boy, he'd give a little squeak of warning if he was going to be naughty!' She rode him in the quadrille at Wembley when he was four. He was naturally well balanced and after only three months training Vicki was riding him in Elementary tests – and this was with Vicki having never ridden a sideways movement before!'

Probably the oldest dressage trainer in the world and probably one of the best! And definitely with an absolutely outrageous sense of fun! Quiet, wicked, but nobody can help loving Herr Rochowansky. Vicki met him when she was twenty-one and he has been the driving force behind her success, so that by 1996 Vicki made her debut in the Olympics. She competed for the British Dressage Team in Atlanta riding Elaine Smith's Dutch Warmblood, Enfant. Vicki had been involved with the horse since he was three, but it was not until he was eight and competing at Prix St Georges that she rode him exclusively. She produced him to

Franz Rochowansky in his later years training Dutchman in piaffe

international Grand Prix level in just fifteen months, which is a meteoric rise for such an inexperienced horse but, as Vicki says, 'He is so incredibly talented with such an elastic, supple way of going.'

1995 was a turning point in Vicki's career. 'After winning the Pas de Deux with Carl Hester at the European Championships, Enfant and I went on to be successful in internationals and won the Prix St Georges and Intermediaire I at the National Championships. We came into the Olympic year with an open mind, we'd had lots of fun and we were ready for Grand Prix, so I thought, "Let's leave it up to Enfant".' Her belief in the horse proved right. Vicki says, 'The Grand Prix test should be the complete test of training. It's quality of gait, quality of mind.'

Vicki has ridden in over forty international competitions on three different horses: Rubens, Vicktor and Enfant. She has been in the ribbons in seventeen British National Championships (on six different horses) and was Intermediaire I National Champion in 1995 and National Advanced Medium Champion in 1997 riding her own Jazz Dancer.

Vicki sees herself first and foremost as a rider. She brands her horses with a lightness and elevation, features that are the essence of all great dressage horses. She loves training young horses. 'They give you food for thought. You never stop learning from them. We start their training making sure they feel comfortable. They work without having to resist the rider, and find their own balance.'

Vicki's advice to aspiring riders? 'Do as you're told!' She laughs, thinking about herself and her lessons with Rocky. 'Go and watch as much as you can. Feed your-self information about every angle of the sport. Go for quality.' A pathway seeker of perfection, striving for excellence: Vicki Thompson is simply exemplary.

RIGHT AND BELOW:
Vicki Thompson
in action

ABOVE: Vicktor was the last horse 'Rocky' trained to grand Prix level. Here we see him showing perfect diagonal pairs in collected trot – a testament to correct training

CHAPTER 3

Flags of Modern Dressage

High dramas have spawned the development of sports dressage – clashes and battles for gold medals, scandals of horses being bought from under the noses of hopeful riders, judges suspected of chauvinism, and even coercions or inducements. In the 1950s the sport became so blighted with corruption that, for a while, dressage hung in the balance as an Olympic sport. Eventually, as in a classic movie, good triumphed over bad, dressage as a sport took root, budded and now flowers more beautifully than ever.

Founded in 1921, the Fédération Équestre Internationale (FEI) takes responsibility for setting standards. It actively encourages competitors to practise similar ways of riding. For instance, in competitions the horses are judged on how they conform to the 'prescribed' standards of:

1. The gaits and their tempos.

2. The movements (for example the canter pirouette).

3. The position of the rider and application of the aids.

4. Self-carriage, submission and the way of going.

If riders deviate from these 'prescribed' guidelines, strictly speaking and provided the judging is consistent, the marks should reflect this; the judges' comments should also point the competitor onto the 'right' path. Setting such standards is essential if we want competitions to be fair. The downside is competitors becoming waterlogged by the stringency of rules (for example, they train only with a view to competing and getting those 'good' marks – and in many instances this has negative effects on the training of horses). Intelligent trainers and riders school a horse in the way that best suits him as an individual and this sometimes means deviating from the 'prescribed' stepping stones of training for a period. However, once the horse is established (and/or for periods of schooling) these creative train-ers will hitch the 'prescribed' competition training techniques onto their own style of training and produce successful competition horses. This ensures that, while their horses are trained according to their individual needs, their training is also in line with FEI regulations.

But for the up-and-coming competitor many factors contribute to making sports dressage rather unclear and tenuous; for example, how fair can judging be? It has been argued that to be fair it is essential:

1. That judges are knowledgeable and trained so they can identify 'good' and 'bad'.

2. That they award marks in a consistent manner.

3. That they are ethical (for example they stick to their principles and are not swayed by their own prejudices, the influences of the media, or riders' reputations.

Considering all the influences thrown into the arena of fairness, the onlooker needs only the tiniest bit of imagination to realise that many aspects can (and do) go wrong. It has to be acknowledged that all factors must be right at precisely the same time for dressage competitions to be absolutely, unquestionably fair. Some-times, the FEI guidelines can go wrong, but generally their effects are positive.

This has not always been the case. General Decarpentry wrote of competitions before the 1930s:

> The horses of the Romanic School showed more willingness than exactitude in their submissiveness . . . On the other hand the German horses evidenced an exemplary submission, a little constrained and sometimes dull, and a strict pre-cision that was more mechanical than animated . . . The judges' differences of opinion were no less sharp, according to the School they belonged to, and the placing of the competitors gave rise to heated arguments.

But as time went by, riders became wiser. Differences and conflicts lessened and later the General observed, 'Year by year, the differences became less pronounced, the styles of both schools more similar, though fortunately for the sake of art, not entirely identical.'

Jane Kidd talks about her concept of the term 'Classical' and its impact on competition. (See also The Great Debate in Chapter 7.) She says: 'The growth of the "Classical School" and development of competitions is very good for dressage. I have loved judging competitions of this type but much of what I saw was not in my view "Classical". The riders might have been trying to follow Classical methods but were not experienced or talented enough to do so. They suffered from the same shortcomings as so many of the FEI dressage riders. There is no big difference between the various schools of training and riding. The main difference is seen in the types of horses, for example the Spaniards on their Andalusians'.

For the first half of the twentieth century, Sweden and France won most of the medals, but since the 1960s Germany has dominated, most particularly with team successes. World-class competitors from elsewhere (for example Christine Stückleberger from Switzerland, Ann-Grethe Jensen from Denmark and Margit Otto-Crepin from France) have had to be content with individual gold medals, because their countries lacked the team power to beat Germany.

The German School has formed its own brand of Classical dressage. Originally coloured by the French and Austrian Schools, and imbedding the techniques into its own 'bedrock' of knowledge, it has become our dream dressage: it provides the answers, it reigns supreme; it is consistent in its results and it spreads expertise to many corners of the globe. A catalogue could be opened to list the records of the numerous successes: names such as Harry Boldt, Josef Neckermann, Willi Schultheis, Uwe Schulten-Baumer, Isabell Werth, Gabriella Grillo, Monica Theodorescu, Sven Rothenberger, Dr Reiner Klimke, Uwe Sauner, Johann Hinnemann, Klaus Balkenhol, Conrad Schumacher, Herr and Karin Rehbein, Nicole Uphoff-Becker – to mention but a few. The annals of these individuals are littered with tales of dedication, perseverance, patience and practise. Spice up these qualities with talent, and the components of competition dressage are activated: the stuff of legends!

A man who rode Grand Prix for Germany and who now specialises in training international riders is Conrad Schumacher. He says: 'German dressage as we know it today came from the cavalry. After World War Two many officers and soldiers, who had been instructors at the Cavalry School, had no job. Because of this they moved further afield, spreading over Germany and becoming the instructors for the riders of the future. German dressage became strong because everybody was taught the same system. There was never any confusion.' He explains the classical influence: 'In the past, handfuls of cavalry officers studied dressage at the Spanish School of Vienna, and obviously when they returned home their accumulated knowledge did influence German dressage, but it never impacted on the training as much as that originated from the School at Hanover. German dressage developed its own methods to suit the needs of the German Warmblood horse.'

Perseverance, patience, practice and talent – the stuff of legends

Isabell Werth on Nissan Gigolo

Karin Rehbein on Donnerhall

Nicole Uphoff-
Becker on
Rembrandt

Anky Van Grunsven on Gestion Bonfire

He says further: 'At the beginning, the final goal should be totally clear in the trainer's mind and that final goal is always the same. But training towards that goal varies because horses are individuals; the trainer is flexible towards each horse and, as he improves, his way of going starts to match the final goal that lived in the trainer's mind at the very beginning.'

Such skills require knowledge, talent, finesse and sensitivity. Conrad's father was ex-cavalry. He possessed an in-depth understanding of people and horses. These factors helped shape Conrad's destiny. In his youth he had the exceptional opportunity to be involved in Dr Neckermann's training stables. Dr Neckermann lives in Conrad's mind as a rider of infinite skill and compassion. He spelt kindness to the horse, so much so, that all his horses were graced with a beautiful and impeccable way of behaving. At the stables, Conrad watched some of the top German riders of that day, names such as Harry Boldt and Reiner Klimke – many of the best were there. Conrad watched them ride, becoming involved in a proactive way by observing and thinking about what passed before his eyes. All this knowledge built the 'rooms' in the house that eventually formed a true picture of dressage for Conrad. He says, 'If you see the best of the best, and you see it a lot, you develop the picture of what you want, what is good; you develop the ability to know exactly what is right and how to achieve it.' This perception of dressage is the highway to success.

Conrad speaks of his role as a trainer: 'I love it! I love to have the responsibility for a rider. Of course, not for ever! When they're younger the trainer has responsibility for everything, but later they take more responsibility themselves; but to teach dressage and to make sure the pupils understand what they are doing and what dressage is about – that is the trainer's job.'

Two of Conrad's well-known students are Sven Rothenberger and Ellen Bontje. Ellen attributes her success to the nurturing and cultivation she has received from Conrad over fifteen years. She now manages his training stables and operates as a respected trainer in her own right. This development of confidence, in both riding and training skills, is not something that grows overnight. It comes through dedication and having the right trainer/mentor to back you through the good and bad times. One tenet of German dressage always remains forthright – the giving of knowledge from trainers to riders and so abilities fuse together to form a wall of unsurpassable excellence.

Conrad explains how he makes dressage simple for the rider to understand: 'The biggest problem in training is that you have to teach feelings, and to teach feelings can be pretty difficult! You can talk about a feeling, the rider can listen, but they don't necessarily understand. For example, if you drink a glass of wine and you talk about the feelings you have as you drink it, it is very difficult to express those feelings precisely – the problem is, you will understand the feeling in a completely different way from another person – and this is exactly the same in dressage. The trainer can be talking, talking, talking, the rider listens, listens, listens, but often does not understand! I try to overcome these misunderstandings by creating situations for the rider so that I can guarantee that they will ride into the feeling I want them to have. and then I say to the rider, "That's it. Don't forget it." My aim is to build the training stone by stone into a house.

'I guide and instruct, that gives you the best measure of both, and it depends on the horse and the rider which way I train. For example, with the more experienced rider I guide and with the less experienced I tend to instruct, but if I have an experienced rider and the situation is such that I have to instruct because something is not right, I give the instruction first – only then can I guide. The rider must be happy to work with me. Of course, if I am teaching someone on a consistent basis and we get to know each other as people I can guide more than instruct. This makes dressage much more pleasant for me, the rider, and the horse. Dressage is all about communication.'

The spirit of innovation was launched by competition. Trainers such as Dr Schulten-Baumer and Sjef Janssen put their own variations on training techniques because they want the horse light, supple and easy to ride. Perhaps such innovations were prompted by the increasing number of women competitors who 'ride-train' their own horses (often big, strong Warmbloods). These women riders tend not to rely on trainers to produce their competition horses, whereas until a few years ago many had their horses schooled for them by male trainers and only rode them for competitions and for short durations. This was not always the case, but frequently so. Now, women have learnt to become good riders in their own right and rely less on the abilities of others. Today, most trainers could be classed as 'guide-mentors' and mostly leave the riding to the competitors. Because women have become more self-sufficient riders, and because they have less muscle power than most men, their horses must go light through technique. Undoubtedly, this has had an influence on training techniques and also on the type of sports horses being bred, with the lighter stamp of Warmblood becoming increasingly popular.

An originator of dressage training techniques that show lightness and elegance is Dr Uwe Schulten-Baumer. He trained his son, also Uwe, to win gold medals for Germany on an outstanding horse called Slibovitz. He has also trained Margit Otto Crepin, Nicole Uphoff-Becker, Pia Laus and the Olympic and World Gold Medallist, Isabell Werth. Dr Schulten-Baumer exercises horses in a round, deep outline, almost a show jumping 'bascule'; they step energetically forwards with their backs lifting and rounding. In an interview with Gabriele Mohrmann-Pochhammer for *Dressage* magazine he says:

> The main point is not the position of the horse's head. The main point is that the muscles of back and neck are relaxed and arch upwards and that there is a supple movement from the horse's hind legs through to the rider's hands, so that the horse can make the best of his natural paces. Most riders and horses find this easier to achieve, if the position of the head and neck is at least temporarily a bit lower. Otherwise, and you see it frequently, horses are pulled together for hours with hollow backs and highly elevated necks, while the riders make intensive use of the whip . . . Many riders only pull the horses' heads down so that the whole weight comes on the forelegs without making the back swing and activate the hind legs. That is of course exactly the contrary of what we want.

Michel Assouline studied with Commandant Saint Fort Paillard of the Cadre Noir. Michel also lived in Germany for a many years and trained with Jurgen Koschel, with Willi Schultheiss and for short time with Dr Schulten-Baumer. It was after his time at the National Equestrian School (at Saumur) that Michel travelled to California to continue his studies with Paillard. He explains why he chose to move over six thousand miles to follow this great rider: 'Paillard had been on the French gold medal winning team in the London Olympics of 1948. He competed in dressage at three Olympics: 1948, 1952 and 1956 and in Olympic three-day eventing. In addition, he taught many American international riders, including Olympic riders.'

Paillard had been Ecuyer at the Cadre Noir in 1939 and for several years afterwards. When he moved to California there was some controversy because he wanted to experiment with different ways of training. For example, he practised the Baucher method, using flexion work and aiming for the horse to be more supple and 'through' in an exaggerated way. But after these experiments he found that the combination that suited most Grand Prix horses was a mixture of the Classical outline (with the poll as the highest point and the horse's nose in front of the vertical) combined with suppling training – in which the horse was ridden in a deeper, rounder outline. Through his experiments Paillard discovered a modern way of training which combines the best of the French and German techniques. His way appears similar to Dr Schulten-Baumer's 'deep' method of suppling the horse.

Michel says: 'Paillard was an intellectual and belonged to the St Cyr School. This is a military School of highly educated individuals and is like West Point in the USA. Trainers like Paillard and Dr Schulten-Baumer are highly intellectual.

Michel Assouline riding Anastasia on the way to winning the Premier League Grand Prix at Etal Manor, May 1998

Great riders are not necessarily intellectuals, but if they are, they can push dressage to wider boundaries of learning.

'Paillard wrote a book called *Understanding Equitation*, which has been very popular in the USA. The book is so different because it is about psychology. Paillard encourages the reader to think why something is not working. By evolving this way of thinking, the rider is enlightened. For example, stiffness can be an effect of the horse not being submissive and may not necessarily relate to suppleness . . . I think the man was so brilliant. He reminded you to focus on *suppling the back and engagement of the hindquarters*.'

Trainers who advocate riding 'round and deep', 'long and low' and 'up and in' have no doubts about the benefits, but warn of the dangers of misuse if ridden incorrectly or for too long a time. Some trainers and judges question the effectiveness of these techniques and say they break the Classical rules of equitation. Their arguments start to fall apart when advocates of these methods produce horses who move in a wonderfully light, elastic way. But there has been confusion as to what is signified by:

1. 'Behind the bit'.

2. 'Overbent' or behind the vertical.

3. 'Long and low'.

4. 'Round and deep'.

5. 'Up and in'.

Kalman de Jurenak, the international trainer (who for many years was responsible for producing young horses ready for the Verden sales) de-mystifies some of the concepts. He says: 'A horse is behind the bit when he won't take the contact. He curls away from the rider's hand and overbends. Such a horse will not "swing", neither will he go forwards properly because he cannot push from behind. The young horse who works with his head put down and even, at times, a little behind the vertical, is quite a different matter. He is not really overbent as long as he takes a contact and steps and swings from his hindquarters. In his working trot, if he steps with his hind foot into his front footprint and swings, that horse is not over-bending, even if he is a little behind the vertical. Such a horse, given a half-halt, pushed up and allowed to step forward, will immediately correct himself and will lighten and take his nose out further. But with an overbent horse you cannot do this. This is the big difference between the overbent horse, which is wrong, and the horse who is lower in front and sometimes a little behind the vertical, but still going correctly through his back.

'Unfortunately, although a lot of people talk about overbending, what they don't talk about is the unbelievable damage that can be caused when a horse goes above and against the bit with his head in the air! The back is then hollow and it is impossible for him to work correctly.' *(From an interview with Pegotty Henriques, 1990).*

Dutchman Sjef Janssen is well known for training Anky van Grunsven. She has won many Olympic, World and European medals and is awarded star billing on television and in national newspapers. In an interview with Bernadette Faurie for *Horse and Hound* he said: 'I don't call my way a system, more a philosophy . . . The main thing about the way I work is that there has to be a clear understanding between horse and rider. If the horse accepts this and responds well, you are already halfway there. Every horse is different. In practice, however, the philosophy is the same, but is adjusted for each horse's individual physical characteristics and movement. You have to be able to read his character and pick up the right signals. If you force him, you will do damage but if you are aware of the signals, the horse will tell you if you are going wrong.'

Regarding Sjef Janssen's 'up and in' way of positioning the neck during training he says: 'Isabell Werth, with her trainer Dr Schulten-Baumer, and Nicole Uphoff-Becker work their horses deep, but it is completely different from the way I work. The one thing we have in common is that everyone is asking the horse to work through the back to be supple.' In 1995 Sjef was voted Trainer of The Year by the International Trainer's Club.

A non-conformist with a wild sense of fun, Sjef is known for his genius. His flair, his way of training, rivals the best; one thing matters to Sjef, training his horses. He hates all medial aspects of life but at the end of the day there's only one thing to do with Sjef – raise your glasses and drink to him!

The world sometimes views German dressage as excellent but austere; a machine gaming to win at all costs, but this image is flawed, because many Germans exhibit a great love for their horses. Most competitors probably say, 'Kindness and flexibility are paramount in training' but the dilemma of every competition rider is that the modern world sees everything from a different perspective. This can impact on dressage training – the demands of competition and the continual striving of modern mankind for quick success can sometimes blight the very routes of dressage, its public awareness becoming tarnished. Competitors can become blinded and think, 'If you get the right results at the end this is less of a worry than how you get there.' But to be *really* successful you must understand that the horse is a living creature with muscles, ligaments, joints and pains. If you keep this in mind and at the same time understand the progression of German dressage through the Scales of Training, you will not go far wrong. (The Scales of Training are explained further in Chapter 4.)

German dressage still predominates, but some of Germany's home-grown experts have thrown nationalistic considerations to the wind, taking their training techniques to an ever-widening audience so that the flags of more nations will unfurl at major events. The competitors prime themselves: now they must excel – more and more – if they wish to achieve ultimate success. Coursing through their minds is the knowledge that only a brilliant performance can win - there is no safe haven for those who seek medals. The rider and the horse, a force together, must take on the world - the rider glorying in the total unity of the moment.

CHAPTER 4

The German Way

LESSON TWO · Training with Ferdi Eilberg

Ferdi Eilberg's first imprinting of German dressage began at sixteen when he worked with Dr Reiner Klimke. Afterwards, Ferdi widened his library of skills with trainers such as Harry Boldt, Johann Hinnemann, Willi Schultheiss and Conrad Schumacher. This bed of knowledge bolstered his own dressage so that nowadays, possessing many talents, he competes internationally and trains international dressage and event riders.

In this section, Ferdi explains how his training links directly to German methods, and most particularly, to the German Scales of Training.

THE GERMAN SCALES OF TRAINING

Ferdi says 'The Germans call them the *Richtlinien* – The Guidelines – the basic scales of training. With them, you take what Nature has given the horse and put it through a system. You use this system to help the horse find his own innate abilities, and these improve as the horse progresses through the six different scales. The *Richtlinien* are as follows:

1. *Losgelassenheit*   **4.** *Schwung*

2. Rhythm   **5.** Straightness

3. Contact   **6.** Collection

Scale 1: Losgelassenheit

The German word for loosening and suppleness is '*losgelassenheit*'; it means to eradicate the muscular stiffness of the horse. *Losgelassenheit* develops the horse so that he is properly prepared for the physical demands of the work stage. All training, whether the horse is novice or advanced, should begin with *losgelassenheit* because only then will the horse be physically capable of:

1. Moving actively forwards.

2. Allowing the energy produced by his hind legs to swing through his back.

3. Engaging his hindquarters and, over a period of time, by combining this engagement with the other five stages of training, being able to shift his centre of gravity so that he carries a larger proportion of his weight on his hindquarters, and not on his forehand. This shifting of his centre of gravity elevates the horse's forehand, and consequently his gaits become more expressive.

Ferdi says, 'It is physically impossible for a horse to give any degree of quality of movement until his muscles have first been suppled and loosened. A sure sign of *losgelassenheit* is when the horse swings through his back and the rhythm of the gaits improves.' *Losgelassenheit* is also known as warming-up. 'How you ride *losgelassenheit* depends on the horse's personality and his standard of training. For example, with young horses as much as 90 per cent of a training session can be devoted to this phase. A supple and calm horse would start in walk on a long rein, usually for five to ten minutes, before being trotted around the arena perhaps in turns and circles. The canter is normally included. But for a hot horse it is better not to insist that the horse stays in walk when he actually wants to get on with things and go forwards. Go off in working trot and let the horse use some of his excess energy and then when he needs a breather, he will be happy to relax and walk on a long rein. With a trained horse *losgelassenheit* normally takes 25–40 per cent of the training session, although this does vary with each horse. Most horses begin with walk on a long rein for about ten minutes; a slow start allows the horse to warm-up gradually. During *losgelassenheit* I ask the horse to stretch his head and neck down so that the muscles along his top line become loosened and suppled. To ask for this stretching the horse is ridden with an extra bit of "roundness" onto the bridle and then the rider lets the reins slip through the fingers and as this happens the horse will want to stretch down. It's his way of saying "thank you". Sometimes, warming-up can take place on a hack. Variety

Horse stretching
down in
losgelassenheit

prevents the horse from becoming bored and encourages him to use himself in
different ways.'

Losgelassenheit overflows into another German principle of dividing each training session into parts:

a. The *losgelassenheit* (as already discussed)

b. Work

c. Relaxing, or cooling off

The Work

'Flexibility is the key element to the work phase. Obviously, it is impossible to
teach a horse everything in one session. Focus on the parts that will benefit the
horse most at that time. For example, a young horse may need to concentrate on
rhythm or straightness, or both, whereas an advanced horse may need perfecting
in the shoulder-in or canter pirouette. Always aim for positive, clear instructions.
Be aware of the maxim, "the right amount of demand at the right moment".

'In the work phase with the trained horse you go through a check-off list as if
you were checking an aeroplane before take-off. Once the basics are ticked off

Young horse in working trot

satisfactorily, bring the horse more together between leg and rein by using changes of gait and the half-halts and only when the level of submission is good, progress to the teaching phase. Tailor the work to suit each horse's rate of development. Most importantly, never move past the basics unless you can honestly say each aspect deserves a tick. Keep in mind that some days the horse can progress quicker than others. The tick-off list prevents bigger mistakes creeping into the training. Catch them early; later they are much more difficult to correct.'

Ferdi advises, 'During the work, sprinkle in moments when you allow the horse to relax, perhaps a circle or half a circle, in walk on a long rein. These breaks give the horse a "breather" and help prevent stressing him beyond his physical capabilities.'

Relaxing or Cooling Off

'This cools the horse off mentally and physically. The aim is to return him to his stable in a relaxed and happy state of mind and body. This will help motivate him for the next training session. Normally, this phase lasts for approximately ten minutes, but the timescale is decided by the needs of each individual horse. In most cases, cooling off is best done by stretching work and/or walk on a loose rein.'

Scale 2: Rhythm

The German translation of rhythm is '*takt*', and this encompasses more meaning than the English word. *Takt* means that the horse moves in a constant tempo and that this tempo is married to the correct, regular footfalls for each of the three dressage gaits of walk, trot and canter. See Table 7 (page 82–83) for a fuller explanation.

'Horses have natural rhythm, some more than others, but they all share one factor in common – as soon as they have to cope with the weight of the rider, their natural balance is impaired. The primary aim of dressage is to re-establish this natural balance under the rider's control.

'You develop a good rhythm by encouraging the horse to accept the forward and restraining aids. During all the dressage training you are constantly fine-tuning the horse's acceptance of these basic aids. I spend a lot of time with my horses, young and advanced, in reinforcing these basics. The horse needs to understand "I must go forwards from the leg", "I must go sideways from the leg", "I must be in both reins", "I must allow the leg precedence over the rein, no matter how much the rein comes on." Always the horse must be in front of the leg. The way of going is paramount to the success of a dressage horse. He can only be as good as the level of his basic work.

'Capturing the horse's natural rhythm is not easy. The rider has to have a "feel" for rhythm. There is a delicate balance between "getting it right" and "getting it wrong" that inevitably comes from under-riding, or over-riding:

1. When under-riding, there is not enough energy coming from the hindquarters to enhance the rhythm and of course the horse will not be in front of the leg or accepting the contact.

2. When over-riding the horse is pushed "over-the-top" of his balance. He will cope with this pressure by speeding up his gaits and/or stiffening his muscles against the demands of too much engagement at too early a stage in his training. Invariably, this leads to him hollowing his back, dropping onto the forehand or coming too strong in the contact.

'All the reactions above put the horse out of balance, onto his forehand, and make it much more difficult for him to move forwards actively in good rhythm. "Throughness" emerges once a good level of rhythm and contact have been achieved. The Germans call it "*durchlässig*" and it is refined and developed as the horse improves his way of going. To promote "throughness" the horse moves so that his whole body is well co-ordinated. He maximises his natural rhythm, accepts the contact and harnesses the energy the rider has asked him to produce. He becomes easier to ride, lighter off the aids, and more expressive and brilliant in his movement. Also, rhythm improves further once throughness is achieved.'

Scale 3: Contact

'Contact is always in front of the seat and legs. The horse seeks a contact with the bit, but it should never be forced or artificially produced. The rider must empathise that the energy starts from the horse's hindquarters and travels, by the appropriate application of the forward and restraining aids, over the horse's back to his mouth.

'With the German Scales of Training, the first principle of contact is that the horse's head is kept straight in front of his shoulders. To give you an example of starting the young horse, the rider uses both reins to make the contact and this gives an even feel on both sides of the horse's mouth to the bit. Sometimes, with a young horse, you can encourage him to seek the bit by holding the reins wider apart and low near the horse's neck. You should always remember that the horse should be *on* the hand as accepting a contact, but not supporting his weight on the hand. The rider needs to be able to control the horse's outside shoulder, especially when asking him to make turns. The horse has to understand that accepting the contact is a stable, even thing. He learns to go "through" and forward and this gives him a feeling for a more centred balance. The horse has support from the rider's leg to the contact and finds that "one line".

'This teaching the horse to go forwards from the leg and then accepting a nice even contact is a most fundamental aspect of training. It is the major stone you lay at the beginning of dressage. The movement is going straight through the middle of the horse, the balance is centred and you get the feeling he is going in front of both the rider's legs and into both reins.

'Gradually, you begin to train the half-halts and through these the horse's energy returns to his hind legs. This energy is not allowed to get away through the front, but if you had left the horse without a contact he would probably have engaged himself with an exhilaration of speed and shifted his balance more onto his forehand.

'Horses can be so different; like people they are completely individual. For example, some horses need more support in the direction of forwardness and others in contact. It depends on what a horse has by nature: his conformation; his character; how he moves.'

Table 7. **The Gaits of the Horse** The Measure of a Dressage Horse is the Purity, Regularity, Correctness and Expression of his Gaits

Quotes in this table are based upon Dr Reiner Klimke's *Basic Training of the Young Horse*

GAITS	SEQUENCE OF FOOTFALLS	TEMPOS WITHIN THE GAITS
	Listen to the horse moving and hear the beat of each gait. Irregularities in the gaits are often caused by incorrect collection or extension, i.e. too strong use of the hand by the rider, over-riding the horse too busily forwards, or through stiffnesses in the horse which havs not been loosened or suppled away through training.	(Tempo gives the measure of speed within each gait. *Takt* should remain constant in each variation of each gait. For example, in collection the horse's legs will be raised higher than in extension but the rhythm stays the same.)
Walk	The horse marches each leg forwards in a four-time rhythm so that four hoof beats can be heard: 1. Right hind foot 2. Right fore foot 3. Left hind foot 4. Left fore foot Two or three feet are on the ground at the same time, so in the walk there is no moment of suspension. Each leg must move forward in the same regular rhythm, the same length of stride, and as in all the gaits, **regularity is essential for a good walk.**	**Free Walk** The horse is given a loose rein so that he can stretch out his head and neck completely free of any restriction from the reins. He should march actively forwards and show free-moving steps that express the maximum ability of his overtracking* without losing the four-time rhythm of the walk. **Medium Walk** This is the natural walk of the horse with a touch more energy and the horse overtracking and on the bit. Dr Klimke gives us his principles of training the walk: 'In the basic training we only ride two sorts of walk – the free walk and the medium walk. In the first year of training we ride the free walk with a long rein. In the second year we develop the medium walk, first when out hacking, then in the school during transitions, leg-yielding and figures.' **Collected Walk** The walk steps have more elevation and do not track up. The horse is in self-carriage with his neck raised and arched depending on his degree of collection and the gait is active and 'light'. Many experienced trainers advise against teaching the collected walk too soon. Dr Klimke explains his thoughts: 'During a horse's basic training I let him walk freely on a loose rein as much as possible. I forget about the extended and collected walk at this stage. I use the medium walk when practising transitions from walk to trot, and vice versa; and from canter to walk, and vice versa, as well as for leg-yielding and riding circles and figures in the arena.' **Extended Walk** The rider allows the horse to stretch his head and neck forward until the top line of the neck is approximately parallel with the ground, however without losing contact with the horse's mouth. The walk strides cover as much ground as possible, that is they overtrack and this activity should be without haste. The regularity of the walk steps must be preserved in the four-beat rhythm. * *Overtracking is where the horse steps so that the hind hoofprints step in front of the front hoofprints. Tracking up is where the tracks of the hind feet cover the tracks of the front feet.*
Trot	This is a two-time movement. For example the horse lifts up his left diagonal pair of legs, but very shortly before he places this diagonal back on the ground again, the right diagonal has also been lifted off the ground. This means that the horse is moving with all four legs in the air for a moment, and in dressage this moment is called suspension. If you listen to the horse moving in trot you can hear two hoof beats. 1. Left diagonal (the right hind and left fore) 2. Moment of suspension 3. Right diagonal (left hind and right fore)	**Working Trot** The working gait is nearly the same as the horse's natural trot except the rider asks for a touch more briskness forwards. Many horses will overtrack, but some will just track up and this will depend on how the horse moves naturally and his conformation. For example, if the horse has a long back he could be an active, good, working trot and be tracking up, not overtracking. The main criteria are that the working trot is swinging through in active, rhythmical steps and the horse remains in balance. **Medium Trot** Is developed through the lengthened trot – this is where the young horse is encouraged from the working trot to take longer, more swinging 'through' steps. In this trot the horse moves with free strides which cover more ground than the working trot, but not quite so much as the extended trot. The horse often finds his balance in this tempo by carrying his neck less arched than in the working trot and with his head slightly more in front of the vertical.

You can gauge if the trot is regular in rhythm if the **period of time** each diagonal is lifted, moved forward and then placed down again is **the same**. Many dressage trainers will 'put the horse on the aids' first in trot, secondly in canter, and lastly in walk. Although there are exceptions to this rule, it is normally followed by those following the established German way of training a horse.

Canter

The canter is often described as 'a series of three bounds', or **a 'jump-like' movement**. If you listen to the horse moving in canter you will hear three beats. For example if the horse is cantering on his left lead this is how he moves forwards:

1. Right hind leg
2. Left hind leg and right foreleg together
3. Left foreleg

Followed by a moment of suspension.

Collected Trot

This trot is taught only after the basic training has been consolidated. Dr Klimke explains 'In the basic training we only need the beginning of collection which we establish with half-halts. It is most important when asking for a half-halt in the trot to give again immediately and urge the horse forward with seat and leg aids to keep the forward movement.' He says, 'In the collected trot the steps are higher, the strides shorter, the hindquarters lower and the neck and head carried higher.'

Extended Trot

Keeps the rhythm of the trot intact, with the horse covering as much ground as possible and lengthening his steps to the maximum of his ability through greater impulsion from his hindquarters. Dr Klimke says, 'To describe the characteristics of the extended trot: the extended trot is the ultimate forward movement in the trot. It shows the highest degree of activity and *schwung* and the highest influence of the rider's forward aids. We consider it a climax and end result of a well-planned and all-round gymnastic education of the horse.'

Working Canter

This is the horse's natural balanced canter with a touch more energy added, with the horse working through to the bit. In tempo it is between the medium and collected canter. Dr Klimke explains how he begins its training: 'The young horse should not be asked for canter until he is truly accepting the rider's aids in the trot. We do not, of course, stop the horse from cantering if he feels like it, either in the arena or when hacking out.' He continues, 'To canter for long does not improve the canter stride. The horse gets tired and loses his *schwung* and the hindquarters are dragged along. Experience shows that the best way to develop the canter is by frequent transitions on the circle between trot and canter.'

Collected Canter

The hallmark of the collected canter is the lightness of the horse's forehand and the engagement of his hindquarters so that his shoulders become mobile and his quarters active. Dr Klimke explains how he develops self-carriage towards the collected canter. 'We use the exercise "stroking the horse's neck". The rider moves both hands forwards so that they are positioned, for a moment, several inches above the horse's mane and halfway along his neck, and during that moment there is no contact with the horse's mouth. This moment, or period of time, is normally for the duration of a canter stride, and afterwards the rider brings the hands back to their original position (which is normally close to the horse's withers), and then contact with the horse's mouth is re-established.' Dr Klimke says, 'We can find out whether the horse is on the outside rein if we move the inside hand forward and pat the neck and the horse remains connected to the outside rein and on the bit.' Also he warns, 'The collected canter should not be part of the programme in the basic training of the young horse.'

He says, 'The breakthrough only occurs in training the canter when the *durchlassigkeit* of the horse has advanced to the point that one can practise the transitions directly from walk to canter and canter to walk.'

Medium Canter

As in the trot, this is the gait between the working and extended canter. The strides cover more ground, jumping more forwards in energetic steps that preserve the three-time rhythm of the canter. The horse remains on the bit, and normally he carries his head slightly more in front of the vertical than in the collected or working canter. Dr Klimke advises, 'It is my experience that the trot and canter strides are best improved when the lengthening and shortening can be practised on long straight lines. It will come more easily and naturally to the horse as it is closer to his natural movement.'

Extended Canter

Preserving the three-time rhythm of the canter, the horse covers as much ground as he possibly can, and lengthens his steps to the maximum of his ability through greater impulsion from his hindquarters. He remains on the bit, although normally he will lower and extend his neck, his head being slightly in front of the vertical.

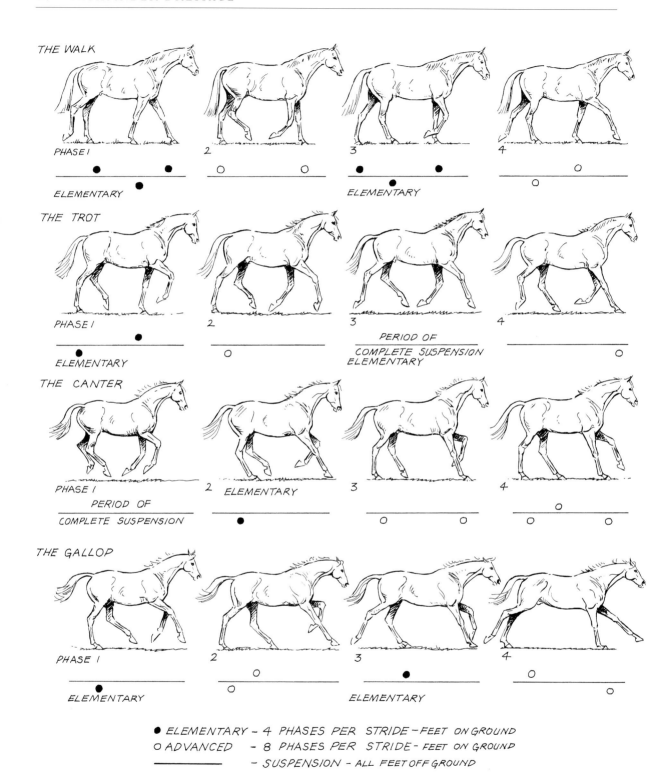

THE WALK

PHASE I   2   3   4

●   ●   ○   ○   ●   ●   ○

●

ELEMENTARY   ●   ELEMENTARY   ○

THE TROT

PHASE I   2   3   4

●   ●   ○   PERIOD OF

ELEMENTARY   COMPLETE SUSPENSION   ○

ELEMENTARY

THE CANTER

PHASE I   2 ELEMENTARY   3   4

PERIOD OF   ○

COMPLETE SUSPENSION   ●   ○   ○   ○   ○

THE GALLOP

PHASE I   2   3   4

●   ○   ●   ○

ELEMENTARY   ○   ELEMENTARY   ○

● ELEMENTARY – 4 PHASES PER STRIDE – FEET ON GROUND
○ ADVANCED – 8 PHASES PER STRIDE – FEET ON GROUND
————— – SUSPENSION – ALL FEET OFF GROUND

The horse in movement, showing the walk, the trot, the canter and transverse gallop

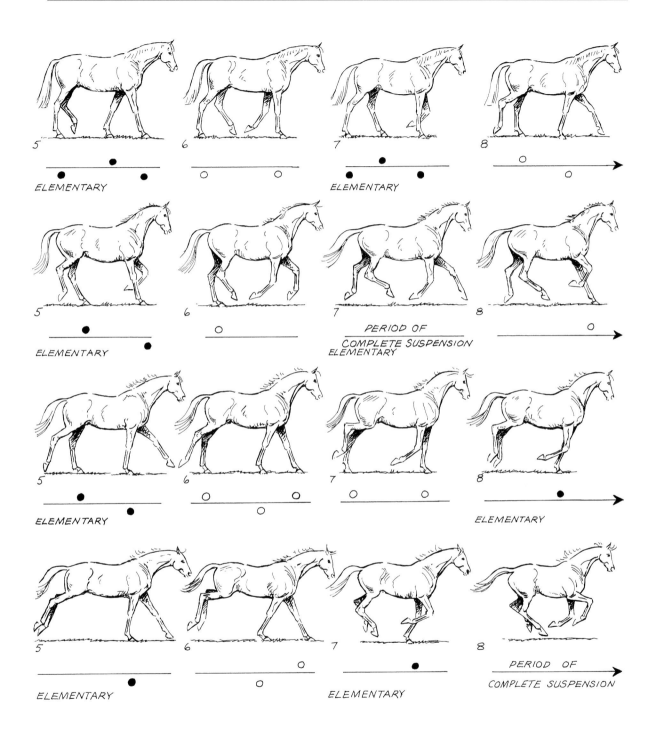

Scale 4: Schwung

Dressage aims to enhance the natural spring in a horse's gaits. Horses running free can be exuberant and show off by dancing. At these moments you can see the 'spring' in their steps. The Germans call it *schwung*.

Once rhythm and contact become established the horse responds more freely between the rider's seat, leg and hand aids. He starts to come *durchlässig* (through) and that is when *schwung* starts to develop. The horse is now capable of carrying more weight on his quarters and the contact becomes more refined.

Some horses are born with less *schwung* than others, and will have less expressive gaits. By improving the elasticity and flexibility of the horse's hindquarters, dressage develops the *schwung* of every horse. But the level of improvement depends entirely on the natural ability of each horse.

Scale 5: Straightness

In dressage terms, no horse is born straight, but we need straightness to lay the building blocks in preparation for the demands of collection. Consistent, true collection is impossible without straightness. Improving and refining the horse's degree of straightness continues throughout his entire dressage life. Without the acceptance of the horse pulling forwards into the rein and moving straight, you're knocking in the dark and hoping somebody's there! Not a consistent way to perform, but if you can use the aids effectively to influence the horse and make him go straight, this is what allows a movement towards perfection; to have a horse looking easy with himself.

'Whether competing or training dressage we are in an arena, a restricted area, and if left to his own devices the horse would cut off corners, lean in, go crooked – but in dressage we have to be more precise and ride straight. It's very important, this feeling, always having the horse between the inside leg and outside rein, because it lightens the horse's inside shoulder and improves the balance.'

Ferdi's Straightening Guidelines

In his straightforward, honest style of teaching, Ferdi uses his own ways of explaining straightening to students. 'I like to use analogies. For example, if you pull a supermarket trolley it is much more likely to move in a straight line than if you push it. To take that analogy further, for the rider it is the feeling of the horse pulling from the hind leg into the rein, and through the rein forwards (a centred-pull-forwards riding); it's a very natural way of making a horse go straight. For example, when in an arena, if the horse wobbles down the centre line, ride him more forwards, put the throttle down a bit, make him "pull" on more and he will automatically come straight – it's a "centred" feeling of the horse going forwards from both legs to both hands.'

The main tools for straightening are:

1. Inside leg to outside rein – which is the biggest influence.

2. 'Centred' riding with the horse 'pulling' forwards (as explained above).

3. Shoulder-fore and shoulder-in (explained in the section on Movements, pp.92–93).

INSIDE LEG TO OUTSIDE REIN

'Begin teaching inside leg to outside rein by riding the horse on a large circle. Initially, keep the same contact on both reins and then start to soften the inside rein with taking and giving of the rein and apply the inside leg a little so that the horse's energy becomes connected to the outside rein. Once developed, inside leg to outside rein can be ridden on circles, turns, corners and when going large. It is the basis of the lateral work.

'In the trot, the centred-pull-forwards riding straightens the horse. However, with the canter it is different because the curl manifests itself more on one canter lead than the other and this makes the canter crooked.' (Curl is where the horse bends his body more to one side than the other, often referred to as the 'stiff' and 'hollow' sides). The moment the horse understands the inside leg to outside rein aids you can start to straighten the canter. Quietly insist that he supports more weight on his inside hind leg. A good way to improve canter crookedness is by riding trot shoulder-in.

'Inside leg to outside rein has to be taught so that it is available whenever you need it, but you should also return to equal contact with both legs and both hands, because ultimately the aim of dressage is to have the horse's energy move straight and equally from both hind legs to an equal acceptance of the contact on both sides of his mouth.'

BEND

'In German we have two words to explain bend. Being precise and separating the neck bend and body bend makes clear exactly what constitutes bend. The German words for bend are:

1. *Stellung*, meaning *flexion* in the neck.

2. *Biegung*, meaning *bend* in the body.

Corners, turns and circles improve bend. On a circle the horse will not achieve straightness without correct *stellung* and *biegung*. The horse is truly straight when he moves straight on a straight line and when the hind feet follow exactly the same line as the forefeet on a curved line.

'As the demands of training progress the rider will notice that the horse may prefer one rein to the other. For example, on the stiff side he doesn't like to bend as much as on his hollow side and so I would ask for more neck bend (stellung) on his stiff side and less on his hollow side. Asking for the opposite of what the horse naturally wants to give straightens out his crookedness and, over a period of time, he becomes equally supple on both reins.'

Scale 6: Collection

'Collection is the increasing ability of the horse to step with his hind legs more under his weight and to lighten his forehand. The steps and strides gain more height through this increased engagement of the hind legs. The stature of the horse grows as he covers less ground and the horse appears to be "going uphill".

'There are different degrees of collection, and even in an Advanced test the degree varies between different movements. For example, there is a higher degree of collection required to perform a good canter pirouette than for a flying change or for a half-pass. The highest degree of collection is achieved in a good piaffe.

'Collection is a gradual process. It relies on the physical development of the horse. The conformation and the gymnastic ability of each individual horse decide how well and how quickly he will learn to collect. As the horse develops and becomes physically stronger the rider can demand more engagement which, in connection with the half-halt, will teach the horse to collect.' (For further advice on half-halts see pp.91–92).

'I sometimes get asked, "Is this collected enough?" The rider can in fact answer this question personally! If the horse is capable of performing a small circle of 6m diameter correctly, in other words, maintaining the size and shape of the circle in self-carriage and with consistent rhythm and fluency, then you will know that the collection is enough! Exercises like transitions, shoulder-in and small circles are helpful to assess and improve the degrees of collection. But do not stay in a high degree of collection for too long without making some transitions forward to a freer tempo. This way you will avoid straining the horse's muscles. It's important for the rider to remember that control in collection comes (when perfected) 80 per cent with the seat and 20 per cent, or less, with the hand – but never more.

'To summarise the importance of The Scales Of Training, they develop the horse to Medium level, but the gap between Medium and Grand Prix is huge. You have laid the basic cornerstones and as the horse gets better these stones become refined like carved stones, and as the horse becomes even better to the ultimate level, you still use the basic stones which were laid at Medium level – The German Scales of Training, the *richtlinien*. This is because most mistakes, including those in Grand Prix tests, are caused by momentary losses of balance, straightness or submission.'

TRAINING THE YOUNG HORSE

'You lay the cornerstones at the beginning of dressage and these are that the horse understands going forwards from the leg and that he accepts the contact. At first the horse has to learn to deal with the rider's weight. Horses react differently to this: some run off, some do not want to go forwards, some fall all over the place for a moment. Once the horse has learnt to deal with the rider's weight you can ask him for free forward movement and as he becomes active in his gaits, introduce contact.

Young horse being lunged in side reins

'Even early on with a young horse you should never feel out of control because this will make him feel even more out of control of himself. Some young horses are quite capable of losing themselves and getting totally carried away in a frenzy of high spirits. The horse has to learn to conquer these feelings. You lay "house rules", you let him know the boundaries of behaviour. You must never feel frightened or threatened by the horse. If this happens you must reiterate exactly the "dos" and "don'ts", and once he is confident and relaxed and comfortable with these guidelines, only then do you allow him greater freedom within those set boundaries of behaviour.

'With a young horse I first ride on the horse's natural balance and teach him to stay in that natural balance as he moves forwards. This prevents him from stiffening against my weight or bearing down onto his forehand. Young horses can be a bit jumpy. Very often they are not steady at accepting the two reins. In these situations, carry both reins a little wider than normal so that it is easier to make contact. Similarly, with turning the horse, help him by moving your hand more to the inside so that he can move smoothly around. But do not pull him on the inside rein because this would unbalance him and make him fall out through the turn. Do not overface him with tight turns, let him gradually make the turn so that he knows which direction he is heading towards and can stay in balance with the movement. Once the horse accepts the two-rein contact the rider can introduce bend.' (As described in the sections on Inside Leg To Outside Rein and Bend pp.87–88.)

'The rider should understand a horse's individual character and behaviour, both mentally and physically. For example, in the early stages of training, a horse can easily reach the limit of his physical and psychological abilities, but as the trainer you have the responsibility to recognise these barriers, and before finishing the schooling demand that bit extra so that you build on the horse's development. However, never be overdemanding.

'Most horses offer what they find easiest and so you can use this knowledge creatively. For example, if you find a horse has a specific problem, think about it and then offer the horse the easiest route to overcome it. If the problem relates to the basics not being taught correctly, return to them and retrain thoroughly before advancing. There is nothing wrong with the horse saying, "I find it difficult but I'll try." You need to be flexible when training young horses and not be overdemanding. You make demands but they must be fair, positive demands so that the horse is challenged and asked to respond.

'In a typical period of training in a month, there may be seven to ten days when you could realistically expect to make clear steps forward in teaching the horse something new. The rest of that time would be spent on reconfirming and consolidating the base of what is already understood. Often, this is how young horses progress. I will give the young horse a break if I feel I have been too demanding; perhaps go hacking for a few days; perhaps jumping or some grid work. This prevents the horse from becoming stale with his work. You know when this happens because the horse almost expects a difficulty. In these situations, think first; be flexible. This makes life much easier for the horse than bullying or grinding through a difficulty. A negative approach will get negative results. Sometimes it is much better to forget a problem for a moment and you will find the horse's mind soon reopens to learning. Problems are often solved by doing something else for a moment (although occasionally you have to stand your ground). It is easy to demand too much, especially with talented horses. You think you can teach something new; speed into the next learning stage; progress at a terrific rate, but this usually end up with skimping on the basics. If a horse excels one day, resist the temptation to expect it automatically the next. It is almost better to switch back a stage, demand less for a few days, and do not expect the horse to be so excellent all the time. Then he will think dressage training is enjoyable.

‘Assess what is going on in the horse's mind. For example, is the horse not doing what I am asking because he is not physically ready yet, or because he does not think it is necessary to make the effort? When you say to the horse "I want this now", he should try to oblige the trainer, but you must also understand that if you get greedy the horse may think the work is overdemanding and suddenly he has a reason to make an issue of it. The rider must know when the horse has given the most he can at that time and praise him, and by stopping at that moment the horse knows he has rewarded himself for his good work.’

THE HALF-HALTS

‘The horse's back acts like a bridge channelling the power from his hind legs to his mouth and the half-halt harnesses that power. The rider gives little half-halts all the time. They are like a conversation with the horse. They refresh impulsion and this energy frees the movement. There are different forms of half-halts, e.g. before a transition, before a circle, a flying change or a canter pirouette. They signal that something new is about to be asked for and they keep a horse's attention and help develop his balance.

‘The moment the horse develops a connection between being forward from the leg to a contact you are able to start the basic half-halts, and these initially are simply transitions from one gait to another or within the tempo of a gait. They say engage more, come back, flex your hocks before you carry on. To summarise, the horse learns to:

1. React promptly to the rider's aids.

2. Handle changes of tempo.

3. Handle changes of gait.

4. Improve his balance.

'In the half-halt, the hand connects the horse on the seat. The hand can be used like squeezing a sponge, or sometimes with a young horse the rider may need to make the message clearer by using the whole of his arm. The amount of leg used depends on the needs of each horse. Understand that any "take" is only 50 per cent of the half-halt; the "release" is the other 50 per cent. The longer you apply the "take", the more likely you are to suffocate the energy. The more smoothly and clearly you apply these aids the better the horse will respond. It is much better to use several little half-halts to give the message to "come back" rather than pulling and constantly holding back the horse, because this suffocates the energy.

'To explain how the half-halt works on the balance of the horse: the "take" part of the half-halt stops the energy of the horse going out the "front door". The moment the energy arrives back to the horse's hindquarters you release the "take" and the contact lightens. This half-halt promotes self-carriage and balance.'

THE MOVEMENTS

'To be good at dressage the rider must develop the skill to know which exercise to use and when to use it to get the right results. The rider must understand that the relationship between the horse's way of going and the execution of the movements is very close.'

Shoulder-In

'This becomes perfected from the horse accepting the rider's inside leg and outside rein. Normally, in competition riding, shoulder-in is shown with a thirty-degree angle and is on three-tracks (the inside hind leg follows the line of the outside foreleg, the outside hind leg and inside foreleg each make a separate track). To explain further, in reality, what appears as enough angle depends on the conformation of the horse. For example, a narrow-based horse (one who steps close) will have to show more angle than a broad-based horse to make a good three-track shoulder-in. In most cases when I first start teaching shoulder-in, I tend to ask for less angle. I am looking for a good quality trot before I ride into shoulder-in, and that the trot rhythm stays consistent. If the horse signals difficulties I make it clear to him that they are easily overcome by stepping more forwards.'

Ferdi explains how to ride shoulder-in: 'Put the inside leg on the girth and ask the horse's inside hind leg to engage more. The outside leg, positioned slightly behind the girth, in a passive, holding position, keeps the quarters on the track.

Shoulder-fore

Shoulder-in

The inside rein looks after the flexion to the inside and a consistent contact is kept with the outside rein.

'The shoulder-in continues as an invaluable exercise throughout the horse's training and can be used as a loosening, suppling exercise as well as a preparation for the more difficult movements.'

Other Lateral Work

Threading through all the lateral work is the acceptance of flexion, bend and forwardness. If these 'threads' are well secured it is rare to get a horse with 'hang-ups' about going forwards and sideways. Ferdi says, 'You profit from the horse having really learnt to go in front of the leg and accept the two reins – then you will rarely have problems such as the horse tilting the head or dropping the outside rein. The rider must understand clearly all the aids for the lateral work and know theoretically and practically when and how to apply them to get correct results.

'Provided that the horse is willing to be positioned by the rider's aids it should be possible to increase the difficulty of the lateral work, for example movements such as travers, renvers and half-pass. Travers and renvers help improve bend and are easier for the horse to perform than the half-pass. Obviously, for that reason, they should be well established on both reins before the half-pass is taught and likewise, the shoulder-in should be good before travers and renvers are begun.

'When you start the half-pass, ask for inside flexion and make a clearer connection with the inside leg and the outside rein. This will bring the horse close to a shoulder-in position and, as you move into the half-pass, lead the horse from the outside rein into the new direction and keep him bent around your inside leg. Your inside leg plays an important role because it maintains the bend and regulates the engagement and cadence.

'The inside rein gives the flexion and lightness; sometimes you may need to refresh it. The outside leg bends the horse around your inside leg and asks him to move sideways. Your weight is more on the inside seatbone because this encourages the horse to step in this direction. Keep in mind that the half-pass is a forward and sideways movement. It may appear parallel with the long side of the manège, but to ensure rhythmical and fluent gaits the horse should move diagonally down the line of the half-pass and this is especially true in the early days of training.'

Problems with flexion normally originate in the poll and are connected with the horse not accepting inside leg to outside rein. There are two types of faults:

Half-pass right

Dropping the outside rein and the poll tipping to the outside (i.e. for left flexion the horse's nose tips to the left and the poll to the right). Ferdi says, 'This fault is easier to solve than the other way around. The horse does not take enough outside contact. To correct it, ask for plenty of flexion to the inside, and as you do so put the outside rein "on" and take the inside one "off". This automatically takes the nose back and makes the poll come over into the flexion.'

The poll overbending and 'rolling' away (i.e. for left flexion the horse's nose tips to the right and the poll to the left). Ferdi says 'This is more difficult to correct because they roll over from the outside rein but are still tipping away. The best way to conquer this problem is to ride with hardly any flexion at all so that the head is nearly straight, and reconfirm the even contact in both reins.

'The lateral ability of a horse never stays exactly the same. Most horses have a basic preference to the left or right side, but this will sometimes change from one side to the other, and so the rider has to be sensitive to any change or variation.'

Table 8. **Assessing Quality in the Half-Pass**

ASPECTS	
	1. The stepping over of the horse's legs must be of a consistent length per step. The gaits must be good, rhythmical and working 'through' and engaged.
	2. There must be a correct and definite flexion in the horse's neck, which should look in the direction of the movement, and the bend throughout the horse's body stays the same.
	3. The balance and fluency of the movement should remain consistently good throughout the entire half-pass and the horse should stay parallel from marker to marker.

'Once all the lateral movements are established they need to be checked for correctness and practised regularly. They play an important part in the daily gymnastic work of the horse. The rider must pay attention to the horse's basic way of going. Any lateral movement can only be as good as the basic gait in which it is performed.'

Extension

'Some horses are more gifted than others in their ability to extend their gaits, but because it is a question of balance and engagement the rider can influence the horse's natural ability quite considerably by consistently improving the lightness of the forehand through engagement of the hindquarters.

'With a young horse, as soon as he can maintain his balance with engagement he will become more and more confident to use the freedom of his shoulder to swing forward with bigger and more rhythmical strides. If the horse needs sharpening up from the leg aids, use transitions within the trot and canter gaits, and/or upward and downward transitions from walk to trot, trot to canter, canter to trot and trot to walk.'

Extended trot: Ferdi Eilberg on Arun Tor

Canter Pirouettes

To start teaching this movement, first check the quality of the collected canter. It should be the case that:

1. The horse engages his hindquarters more under the body through increased flexion of the hocks.

2. He lightens his forehand in each stride of the canter.

3. The canter is straight.

'I prepare the horse for the demands of the pirouettes by transitions from walk to canter and canter to walk and to improve the "sitting" of the collected canter which increases the degree of collection, I ride transitions within the collected canter to a higher degree of collection, but I only do this exercise for a short time. Other exercises include simple changes, small canter circles and counter-canter and travers canter.

'Once I am happy with this work I begin by riding travers on a large circle. I feel how the horse copes with this exercise and practise it over a fair period of time, perhaps several months. All the time, I am concentrating on its improvement and ensuring that it is equally good on both reins. I prioritise and constantly check that I have quality and consistency on a bigger scale, and only then do I consider taking the travers circle to a smaller size.

'The rider must understand that just because the horse can do travers on the circle, the real canter pirouette does not happen instantly. Once the horse is strong enough, the quarter-, then the half- and finally the full pirouettes can be taught. You should always be sure of the quality of the canter and only ask for the circle to come smaller when a good canter can be maintained. Once you start to ask for the pirouettes it is important that you feel you are taking part in every stride of the canter and that you can look after the horse's position, balance and activity. This is essential because if the horse is left to himself, he would hurl himself round the pirouette, but in training we are managing the canter so that the horse performs the canter pirouette in balance. The horse has to learn to turn within that good balance and should not resort to emergency turns. Throughout all this training I look at the canter pirouette as being nothing more than riding a good quality canter around on a spot and I keep the same control that I would expect in a collected canter going forwards on a straight line.'

Left canter
pirouette

Right canter
pirouette

Flying Changes

'These can be taught once the horse is capable of giving a nice collected canter and the horse can clearly identify between left and right canter. When you ask the horse for his first single flying change you have to feel that he has a good chance of obliging you. Be sensitive to the natural abilities of each horse and to the quality of his gaits. Sometimes when starting the single flying changes it is better to practise them and then leave them for a time and return to more simple work. When you return to teaching the changes again you should find the horse copes more easily, and this enables you to take them a step further.'

Ferdi talks about how he teaches the one-time flying changes: 'It is important to stress that the horse should be confirmed up to, and including, two-time flying changes. At these levels the horse still has time to rebalance himself and there is time for the rider to regain control if the balance is lost, but in the one-time changes there is no chance for this – the horse has to stay in balance while he "jumps" the changes. The demand from the balance is quite different from the four- three-, and two-time changes. The horse should be given time to learn this

Flying change left

Flying change right

new one-time flying change balance and so I slowly introduce its demands by first asking for "one-two" changes.' (This is where the horse jumps into a change and immediately follows it with another change, i.e. two one-time changes). 'After this I allow the horse to regain his balance completely and check that he is listening to the leg before I repeat the exercise. Slowly I build on this by riding "one-two-three" one-time changes and eventually I can ride the exact number of one-time changes I require, but all the time, the balance has to stay absolutely clean.

'If neither student nor horse have ever done one-time changes before I will train the horse in the movement myself. This is because while the horse is still "fragile" in the one-time changes a less experienced rider could disturb his confidence. Also, there are slight variations in how each person applies the flying change aids, and each horse becomes adjusted to one particular rider's way of asking, so it is not fair to the horse to expect him to have two people riding this new movement at the same time. However, once the horse is reliable and confident in his one-time changes then the student can have a go at riding them.'

Teaching the one-time changes takes tact and feel. The rider must be knowledgeable and capable of co-ordinating the flying change aids precisely.

Piaffe and Passage

Ferdi will often ask for the first stages of piaffe (known as the half-steps) early in the horse's education, however only when the basics are established. 'Piaffe confronts the horse with a high degree of discipline, and because of this I ask myself "Is the horse ready for this discipline? Is it going to be constructive to his development to teach it at this stage of training?"

'Initially, I walk the horse in-hand and in this work I establish a degree of control, a respect that is similar to that needed when riding. This is achieved through simple in-hand exercises such as walk on, halt, rein back a few steps. The horse has to look to me and respect what I am asking him to do. He must not walk into my space, mow me down or charge off! Once this control is guaranteed, I ask him to move from the four-time rhythm of the walk, through increasing its activity, to the two-time rhythm of the trot for the half-steps.

'Teaching the piaffe is very much a matter of feel. In the half-steps the horse has to cope with being more active from behind, but at the same time, not allowing that forward energy to move away. He may occasionally perform piaffe-type steps on his own accord, but it is harder for him to know what to do when the trainer asks him for piaffe. The trainer is saying: "Go forwards, but stay in one place." This is why the half-steps and piaffe work increase the submission of the horse. You have to spend longer with some horses than others. These types have to learn to relax and become confident that you are not getting after them. They have to figure out what you want, and this can take time. Other horses respond willing and will quickly offer a few steps. Of course, as a good trainer you would not exploit this talent by doing too much. You know that by playing with the half-steps, leaving them for a time, when you come back to them they will be better and easier. I often find that having trained the half-steps the horse's other work

Piaffe

improves. The reason being he has figured out for himself that the demands of submission and discipline can really be quite easy. He grows in confidence, and this spills out into the quality of all the training.

'The best way for the rider to learn the feeling for piaffe is by riding horses who are experienced in the movement. For this reason, only consider teaching a horse the half-steps under the supervision of a knowledgeable dressage trainer.

'The passage is more physically demanding than the piaffe. For this reason I teach it later in the horse's development, and never ask for it until the horse's body and athleticism have built up. The difficulty is, if you ask a horse to passage when he's not developed in his muscles and quarters, you risk "pushing him apart". Teaching the passage is like piaffe, it is a question of feel. I feel when the horse is ready for passage and this is normally when his collected trot becomes so established that he finds it easy to push off the ground with more spring and balance when I ask him.'

FERDI EILBERG'S TRAINING TIPS

No Guarantees 'There are no guarantees with horses. Most want to try and please their handlers. Some are confused and need to be shown the way. Others are unsuited to dressage physically and would be better off specialising in another discipline.

'Occasionally I train a horse I have to change my mind about, for example the horse I think will turn out really talented doesn't grow into his talent and the horse I think might be average turns out to be very good. Dressage is full of surprises and you must be flexible in your training and, if necessary, be prepared to change your approach.'

Break Monotony 'I like to give all my dressage horses a break from just dressage, so that they stay happy and fresh in their minds. I am always looking for ways to avoid monotony and because I have show jumped in competitions and enjoy it, I jump all my youngsters and also some of the advanced horses.

'All the horses are hacked down a quiet lane, often to loosen up or cool down. It does not matter what stage of training they are at, varying the work keeps them using themselves in a different way. It opens their minds to something more than just going round and round in circles.'

Avoid Ruts 'It is easy for humans to get stuck in a rut. I find sometimes that a different feel with a horse can break a deadlock. For this reason I like to watch horses being lunged or being ridden by a capable rider. This perspective keeps my eyes open so I have the chance to avoid those ruts!'

Improve upon Deficiencies 'A good way to train is to identify the main deficiencies of the horse, because they indicate what needs to be improved. You should aim to improve those deficiencies to a reasonable level.'

Developing Feel 'The rider has to be primed to lift subconsciously learnt "feel" into the conscious mind, because only then can intelligent decisions be made as to when something is right or wrong, and when the moment is right to correct it, or allow more, or demand more.'

Be Open-minded 'I follow the traditional German way of training horses. I avoid training in any one specialised discipline too early. I bring up my youngsters in a broad spectrum of skills – this complexity of training normally includes cross-country, show jumping, lungeing and dressage. As a horse progresses he may start to show talent in dressage and, at that point, I will begin more specialised dressage training and begin his dressage competition career.' Ferdi advises: 'Be open-minded. Allow the horse the opportunity to show you which channel he should follow. Give him the chance to display his best abilities.'

FERDI EILBERG'S PROFILE

For several decades now we have seen Ferdi as 'tops' as a successful international dressage rider – a long trek from his childhood, when his greatest joy was to ride bareback through the countryside of Niederzeuzheim in Germany.

Ferdi possesses that brand of confidence that only grows through proving your ability. Totally professional, he sets himself high standards and only tolerates 100 per cent success. Ferdi says, 'I like to get things right. My aim is to do the horses justice and to bring them on as best I can. I like to put up a creditable performance.'

He talks about his early years as a rider. 'I did a swap with a friend so I could ride this beautiful Thoroughbred stallion! I had a school friend who wasn't keen on the lunge lessons his father had arranged and so I gave him sweets in return for the lessons. At the same time, I was riding regularly at a trekking yard and so I rode lots of different kinds of horses. The first horse I owned was with my sister, a good-looking Warmblood called Anchero. He had to do everything, but I also competed him in Advanced dressage and he was the first horse I trained to Grand

Extended canter: Ferdi Eilberg on Arun Tor

Prix. Of course, my sister got the odd ride too!' (Besides his success in dressage Ferdi has also show jumped to Grade A level.) Since those early days, Ferdi has trained many dressage horses to international Grand Prix – most notably Giovanni, Arun Tor and Broadstone Demonstrator.

His serious dressage training began as a boy of sixteen when he went to work for Dr Reiner Klimke and studied for his *Bereiter* examination – the first qualification towards the higher *Reitlehrer* qualification – which he passed in 1978. He stayed working with Dr Klimke until he was twenty and travelled with him to many major shows, including grooming for him at the 1972 Munich Olympics. Ferdi considers Dr Klimke to have been one of the ultimate riders of our time: 'He achieved so much. For me, he was an all-round horseman. What helped me when I was studying with Dr Klimke was watching how determined he was to find a way to turn horses around and make them work for him. He was very focused.'

Ferdi Eilberg's mentor, Dr Reiner Klimke, on his great horse, Ahlerich

In 1979, Ferdi married his English wife, Geri. They moved to England in 1980 and shortly afterwards Ferdi was selected as the key player in the Dalgety Spillers project. This was a form of sponsorship created to promote British dressage riders, but unfortunately the Fund folded after eighteen months as a result of company politics. Initially, this proved a setback for the Eilbergs, but in reality was a silver lining to their dressage horizons because it prompted them to buy Pink Green Farm. Near Redditch, England, this was a splodge of derelict farm buildings in 1984 but some time later, after lots of hard work, the Eilbergs transformed the farm into a dressage oasis; an idyllic setting to train and promote national and international riders and horses.

Being issued with a British passport in September 1990 opened up the avenue for Ferdi to represent Great Britain internationally. 'I'd always said that if I had a horse good enough to be a real winner I'd change my citizenship.'

Ferdi talks about one of his special horses, Arun Tor. 'At seventeen, he's approaching the last of his competition years, but in many ways they have been the best. It's only since 1995 that I've been able to ride him to the edge; that I can walk the tightrope with him.' By Osberton Napoleon out of a Thoroughbred mare, Light Our Lady, Arun Tor stands like a great war-horse, measuring a full eighteen hands high. His lovely, rhythmical gaits add to his rare combination of power and sensitivity. Developing such a powerhouse has taken time and patience, and has probably been Ferdi's biggest training challenge. 'I caught glimpses of Arun's qualities when I watched a student ride him. He was a young horse of five at the time and had hardly done anything, but when I rode him for the first time his abilities were confirmed by the feeling he gave me.' After sixty-seven major successes this gelding has certainly earned his daily ration of oats. With a kind temperament to match, he has on occasions been ridden by Maria Eilberg, Ferdi's teenage daughter. A modest man, Ferdi would be embarrassed to admit to his reams of astounding successes and the ways in which he has helped students – particularly through difficult times – so they, too, could sachieve successes.

Ferdi believes in 'slaying the dragons' of your doubts or fears and leaving the doors open to learning, always giving the horse the chance to shine through with his talents. His homage to the horse can only be equalled by the homage due to his skills as a Maestro.

Ferdi riding Broadstone
Warianka - a horse for the
future

Ferdi Eilberg's Competitive Highlights

1986	1st	Aachen Grand Prix Kür riding Giovanni. Ferdi says, 'This was such a victory for me because I won over a rider I really respect, Dr Reiner Klimke. Also, having been in Aachen since 1970, first as a groom and then as a trainer, it was great to ride there and lead the prize-giving into the main stadium just before the finale of the World Show Jumping Championships. The stands were packed and it was a truly memorable occasion.'
1988	Silver	British Team Silver Medal at the European Championship in Lipica riding Arun Tor.
1993	1st	Rennes CDI Grand Prix Special (Arun Tor).
1994	2nd	Volvo World Cup at Wembley (Arun Tor) by a slim margin behind Sven Rothenberger.
1995	3rd	With British Team at Aachen CHIO (Arun Tor).
	1st	Rennes CDI Grand Prix Kür (Demonstrator).
	2nd	Rennes CDI Grand Prix Special (Arun Tor).
	1st	European Championships Grand Prix Kür (Arun Tor).
1996	2nd	Hickstead CDIO Grand Prix Special (Arun Tor).
	1st	Addington National Medium Championship (Broadstone Warianka). This grey mare could be Ferdi's hope for the future. He enjoys training young horses and says, 'For me the fun of dressage is not just the competing but producing, training and riding talented young horses.' Ferdi was awarded a three-year-old potential dressage horse by *Dressage Horse International* for gaining the highest percentage (70 per cent) at the championship.
		Short-listed with Arun Tor and long-listed with Demonstrator for the 1996 Olympic Games in Atlanta.
1997	3rd	Rennes CDIO France, Grand Prix British Team Test (Arun Tor).
	2nd	Hickstead CDI Grand Prix British Team Test (Arun Tor).
1998	3rd	Shearwater 6-Year-Old Potential International Horse Championship at Hickstead CDIO (Highlander).
	8th	British Team at World Equestrian Games in Rome (Arun Tor).

LEFT: Ferdi competing on Tapster, who gave Ferdi's student, Lindsay Jenkins, her first chance of riding Grand Prix

Ferdi Eilberg's Training Highlights

1978	German *Bereiter* – first qualification towards *Reitlehrer* qualification.
Late 1970s	German *Reitlehrer-Abzeichnung* – a Gold Medal award for success in both show jumping and dressage at advanced level.
1984	Official dressage coach for the British three-day event team at Los Angeles Olympic Games.
1992	Official dressage coach for the British three-day event team at the Barcelona Olympic Games.
1980 – present	Ferdi has earned many accolades in teaching dressage – with enough famous pupils to start his own international team! Riders such as: Stephen Clarke with Becket, Jennie Loriston-Clarke with Dutch Courage, Diana Mason with Prince Consort, Young Rider Lucy Farrer on Giovanni, and event riders Mary Thompson, Richard Meade and Captain Mark Phillips and many more . . .
Over 10 years	The international rider Lindsay Jenkins has trained with Ferdi for over ten years. He gave Lindsay her first opportunity to ride Grand Prix with a horse Ferdi trained from the beginning, the chestnut stallion Tapster.
For many years	Ferdi has trained Olympic and World Games event rider Mary Thompson. His creative and flexible input to training her event horses has often greatly improved her success in eventing dressage.
	Ferdi has imparted many words of wisdom to Japanese Olympic and world-class rider Mieko Yagi. She has been training with him for many years now. This combination go on record for the distinction as student/trainer competing against each other at a World Games (Rome Equestrian Games 1998). Historically they are probably unique in this respect.
	Ferdi has been helping his wife with dressage since the late 1970s. Geri is directly responsible for producing their daughter Maria to ride in the British Dressage Junior Team in 1998 and 1999. Now that Maria's skills are advancing, Ferdi will start to take a more active role in her dressage training. Perhaps the time is ripening for another father/daughter dressage duo to emerge?

CHAPTER 5

The Dutch Way

This chapter discusses two Dutch ways of training, the first with Bert Rutten and the second with Jane Bredin which is based on her knowledge of Sjef Janssen's methods. Dutch dressage has grown through Classical and competition influences. Top German trainers have given a competitive edge to the country's international performances. Combining this with Dutch innovation in training methods and natural talent has elevated Holland to a force to be reckoned with. Dutch dressage today is a heady cocktail of talents.

LESSON THREE · Training with Bert Rutten

This Dutchman oozes impeccable integrity. He takes four hundred years of dressage knowledge and blends it with up-to-date ideas. This creates a distinctive, vibrant way of going – Modern Classical dressage. 'The wheel of dressage can never be reinvented,' Bert Rutten says. 'But riders do add their own variations of the same theme, the Classical.'

To give the reader a feel for his training methods, Bert rides two horses, one Elementary and one Grand Prix, and takes them through a typical training session. The basics of his training are:

1. 'Make sure the horse is "on his own legs" (he is in self-carriage and does not lean on the rider's hands).' To teach self-carriage Bert suggests:

   a. 'Ride frequent transitions from one gait to another.' Students say of him, 'Transitions are his obsession. You ride a hundred transitions per session, that is okay, but never less!'

b. 'Ride transitions within the gaits, e.g. collected to medium trot.'

c. 'Ride half-transitions. The rider does this by asking for a transition but, just as the horse engages, it seems to him that the rider has asked him to continue moving forwards. This energises the horse's "engine" and brings the balance more onto his hindquarters, lightening his forehand – in this activated gear he moves forwards in a more expressive way.'

d. 'Once the transitions and half-transitions are perfected the rider can start to sprinkle in half-halts. They engage the horse in a more subtle but direct way than transitions and are the ultimate test that the horse reacts positively to leg, seat and hand aids.'

2. 'The rider is always evaluating the horse's way of going and, if the basic work is not up to scratch the rider carries on refining it. The rider understands that the movements are only as good as the basic work.'

Bert Rutten, whose training symbolises Modern Classical dressage

3. 'Be consistent. Consistent in every way you train the horse. The horse then learns these consistent messages. He gains confidence through knowing the rider always applies them in the same way. There is never a moment when the horse feels as if he has been dumped in no-man's-land and does not know what the rider wants. Good communication with the horse primes him for success.'

4. 'Figuring out the cause of a problem and its effects gives the rider answers to training problems. For example, if the horse makes a mistake, the rider asks 'why?'. Let's consider this scenario: a young horse strikes off onto the wrong canter lead and because he becomes unbalanced, he gets nervous and rushes off in the canter. He thought the rider meant counter-canter because of the way the aids were applied, but really true canter was wanted. A rider who thinks through *cause and effect* will realise the mistake originated from the aids, but a rider who blames the horse and reapplies the canter aids too strongly to reprimand the horse could unbalance and upset him even more. The horse may begin to perceive counter-canter as a difficult exercise and become tense and resistant in this work. Counter-canter has become a problem. Handled correctly the mistake could have been put right before it escalated into a problem. The thinking rider aims to steer clear of these misunderstandings. Repeating mistakes trains problems into the horse. The rider has superior intelligence to the horse with the responsibility to think through gaps in communication and avoid counter-productive situations. The good rider knows brain power is essential to effective training.'

5. 'Repetition is important to good training. The rider repeats the training in a consistently good way and so the horse's dressage improves.'

6. 'I like the horse's way of going to be so well established that it appears to have originated in the mind of the horse. Then I know that his psyche has absorbed the training so completely that no physical or mental effort seems to have been directed by the rider. The aids become invisible and real harmony exists between horse and rider. This to me is good dressage.'

7. 'I educate the rider's seat by progressing the rider's experience, and as the horse comes into better balance the rider's position becomes better. This is because fifty per cent of the rider's position depends on the balance of the horse. If the focus is too much on perfecting the rider's seat, before the horse is well balanced, the rider often stiffens against the horse. By allowing the rider's position to develop gradually through practice and correct repetition, the seat becomes consolidated and grows into a "feeling" seat that is sensitive to the needs of the horse.'

TRAINING AN ELEMENTARY HORSE

Walk

Each schooling session begins with walking the horse on a long rein. The free walk is changed to medium walk and normally includes lateral work such as shoulder-in and half-pass.

Trot

The horse becomes concentrated on his work and this enables him to respond easily to the rider. To achieve this, his character must be considered. For example, the lazy horse is ridden 'off the leg and seat' so that he becomes 'in front of' the forward signalling aids. This is best achieved by riding plenty of transitions, especially transitions within the gait, but also trot to halt. The 'hot' horse is ridden quietly so that he feels comfortable with accepting the leg, seat and hand aids. Transitions from a soft trot to a working trot help, and also trot to halt. Medium trot is introduced when the horse is relaxed and happy on the aids.

Lateral work is introduced into the trot work. Three-track shoulder-in and the half-passes are ridden, but with less difficulty than those asked of a Grand Prix horse. For example, the half-pass is taken down the centre line, returning to the track whereas, with the Grand Prix horse, it might be ridden across the whole diagonal of the arena. The Elementary level horse must show good angle and bend in the half-pass.

Canter

Like the trot, the canter is ridden according to the horse's temperament. The emphasis is on putting the horse 'on the aids'. The picture should be that the canter moves actively forwards through to the bridle. To ensure straightness and because the canter is prone to crookedness, Bert often trains in canter shoulder-fore along the track on both reins.

Bert is always searching for the easiest, simplest way to teach the horse new movements and this will help advance the Elementary horse to the next level of dressage. For example, with an established Elementary horse, Bert might teach the single flying changes or the beginnings of the canter pirouettes. For this, he collects the canter and then works the horse in travers position on a large circle. As the horse becomes able to maintain good balance, this travers circle is made smaller, perhaps to 10m. This prepares the horse for the canter pirouette, but at this stage, and until the horse is strong enough in his back and limbs, the true canter pirouette is not ridden.

Bert training a student in shoulder-in... and half-pass

'Essentially the rider must understand: new movements are never taught at the expense of detracting from the quality of the basic gait! This is very important to understand.

'Most of my training consists of simple work, fine-tuning the basics, transition work and putting the horse on the aids. I want him to progress, but I only teach new movements when the horse feels right.' Knowing when the time is right, when the 'feels' are right is quite a skill and is the reason why having an 'eye' on the ground – a good trainer – is fundamental to good dressage.

Rest

Periods of rest on a long rein are interspersed into the training session for a few minutes at a time.

The Flying Changes

For the changes the horse must be well engaged, secure and responsive to the canter aids. Bert checks that the Elementary horse he is teaching is well prepared by riding in a canter 'gear' somewhere between collected and working canter. He often prepares the horse with canter shoulder-fore exercises which straighten the canter (an essential for flying change work). Once Bert is happy with the horse's responses, he double-checks the canter is moving actively forwards, because only then will the horse jump cleanly into the changes. The canter must be really 'true', stepping through with spring and vibrance.

Returning to The Trot

Transitions! Transitions! Bert checks that the horse is in self-carriage and 'light on all four legs'. This work normally includes transitions from working to medium trot and trot to half-transitions.

Returning to The Walk

Every dressage session is finished with walk on a long rein. The horse is encouraged to stretch his head down and to step forwards in a free walk. The horse has been supple and relaxed throughout the entire schooling period. On many occasions he will also be cooled off on the horse walker for a while and he will have been warmed-up in the same way. The same rules apply for the Grand Prix horse.

The whole training session has lasted one hour, fifteen minutes: twenty minutes in walk warming-up and cooling down, ten minutes in walk rest periods and forty-five minutes in trot and canter. The horse has been in consistent work for two years and is fit and healthy.

For the Elementary horse Bert focuses on:

1. Keeping his mind happy and alert.

2. Improving his balance.

3. Guiding him towards a better degree of self-carriage.

4. Progressing him to the next level of dressage.

TRAINING A GRAND PRIX HORSE

Walk

The session normally begins with ten minutes of walk, including shoulder-in, travers, renvers and half-pass. The aims are to encourage calmness but responsiveness, relaxation, suppleness and attention to the rider's aids.

The quietness of walk supples the older horse without putting strain on his limbs. He is given the chance to find his posture in preparation for the effervescence of the faster gaits of trot and canter.

Trot

The trot is often polished by riding a soft trot and using transitions to walk, half-transitions and half-halts. Lateral movements are interwoven into this work. These exercises steadily loosen the horse into a fuller trot, and this may eventually be ridden into extended trot depending on the 'feel' of the horse.

Bert's technique for riding shoulder-in is a good example of how he teaches all his work. He believes that the laws of Nature lay the guidelines and that suppleness can never be achieved artificially or with force. For the shoulder-in, Bert asks the horse into a shallow angle which is just slightly more than shoulder-fore and so gradually, the horse becomes more suppled and more bent around the rider's inside leg. Only when he feels like this is he asked to give the three-track shoulder-in, because only then is he capable of giving it correctly.

Bend should run equally through the entire length of horse's body, not just from his head and neck. To explain this more fully: in circles, turns and lateral work, if the horse is to remain 'straight' he has to stretch one side of his body more than the other, and if too much neck bend is demanded without the corresponding bend through the horse's body, stiffness and crookedness result.

The horse is prepared for all the movements. He is set up physically in readiness for their demands, because only then will his muscles be relaxed and well co-ordinated and only then will he be able to respond to the rider's instruction in the right way.

In all the movements Bert concentrates on the quality of the gaits, balance and the horse's willing acceptance of the bridle.

Canter

Collected canter is started, with frequent transitions to walk. Cantering shoulder-fore helps ensure that the canter is straight. Half-passes are taken diagonally across the school. Transitions from collected to medium canter follow.

This period of canter lasts for about ten minutes. The horse is light on his feet and working correctly through his body in the transitions and half-halts; he remains soft on the bridle and the canter springs forward with good balance.

Rest

Periods of walk on a long rein are given as a 'breather'. Always, the rider makes sure that the horse is never driven beyond endurance and that dressage is enjoyable.

During these rest periods, Bert thinks about the quality of the work just done, this checks that the horse is improving correctly. After considering all the factors, Bert will tailor the remainder of the lesson to suit each individual horse. For example, if the work has been good, he progresses to more difficult movements, such as the canter pirouettes, piaffe and passage. If Bert doubts the quality of the work, in any aspect, he frequently carries on riding the basics throughout the whole training session.

Canter Continued

This Grand Prix horse has performed well and so after a rest period Bert continues him in the canter. Starting with collected canter and transitions from canter to walk, he then works on the canter pirouettes. For this he rides on a small circle in a slight travers position, and gradually, as he feels the horse can cope with the balance, the circle is made smaller and then smaller, until it becomes the smallest size needed for the canter pirouette. Not many pirouettes are ridden because they can overtire the horse, and if overdone can strain his muscles and joints.

The canter pirouettes have also gone well. Feeling the moment is right, Bert rides the horse forwards into single flying changes. Satisfied that these are jumping through correctly, he adds the sequence changes of four-, three- and two-time. These also go well and so he returns to schooling the one-time flying changes.

Passage

Bert often asks the horse for a continuous 'soft' passage. He says, 'I only ask him for the classically correct passage occasionally. The horse has to be very strong in his back to do the passage well and I want to keep the horse happy and content in his passage work.'

Piaffe

The horse piaffes from the walk, and in different places in the school. He should find it easy, enjoy it and show no resistances. This section lasts for a few minutes – although this may be longer with a well-established Grand Prix horse.

Returning to Canter Again

The horse is asked to repeat the collected canter to walk transitions. Sometimes, if he is performing really well and is not tired, a few more canter pirouettes and one-time changes are added. As the horse strengthens, the canter is required for longer periods and in different ways. With the Advanced horse the canter takes on more significance, and as his fitness and stamina improve he is able to maintain a refined way of going.

Cooling Off

The horse is cooled off in walk on a long rein in the same way as the Elementary horse. The total dressage session for this Grand Prix horse has lasted for eighty minutes, thirty of them being in walk. The horse is fully fit and is being prepared for international Grand Prix competition.

Bert talks about how he likes to train people: 'A trainer and rider relationship should be on a one-to-one basis. You should be friends, not "I'm the instructor, you obey!" An imaginary line joins up the trainer, the rider and the horse. All three should feel they are pulling towards the same goal. This frankness keeps communication free-flowing.'

For more information on Classical riding Bert advises reading *Riding Logic* by Wilhelm Museler and *The Complete Training of Horse and Rider* by Alois Podhajsky.

Vicki Thompson training her horse Jazz Dancer in the canter pirouette. Bert Rutten is Vicki's competition trainer, and helped prepare her for the 1996 Olympic Games

BERT RUTTEN'S PROFILE

Bert Rutten is acclaimed internationally as a talented rider, trainer and breeder of dressage horses, but his modesty would never allow him to brag of these successes!

Bert has competed at world-class dressage shows: he rode Robbi into 10th place at the 1976 Toronto World Championships and competed internationally with other horses such as Parcival, Zirkoon and Garibaldi. He was selected as a Dutch Team rider for the 1984 Los Angeles Olympics. His father, Jo Rutten was also selected – Bert on Parcival and Jo riding Ampère as a reserve. Unluckily for Bert, Parcival went lame, which meant that father had to step into his son's shoes. They are one of the few father and son combinations ever to compete at the Olympics.

Bert started riding when he was nine years old. He has ridden many ponies and horses of all different types and characters. Bert recalls: 'In the early days it was often horses that could buck and rear!' His father has helped him with his riding since the very beginning and Jo still keeps a watchful eye on him today.

Jo trained with Ernest Von Loon, who was a well-known Dutch trainer, and the three-day event rider, Wiel Hendrix. In the 1960s he gave up the sport and probably would never have taken up the reins again if not for his son's enthusiasm for dressage. Even years after retiring from riding, Jo sees one of their stud's horses, smiles and says, 'That's a horse I'd like to ride. He looks so good he makes you want to get back in the saddle again.' Bert explains, 'The good ones are such a joy to ride, so soft-mouthed, so comfortable to sit on, so easy.'

For several decades Bert and Jo have run their stud and training stables in Holland, the Rutten Stables. They specialise in producing top-class dressage horses. Bert says, 'Today in Holland breeders are restricted to using artificial insemination because this limits the transmission of equine sexual diseases, but things were not always this way'. He is talking about one of their top stallions, Clavecimbel. 'When we bred naturally, he really adored one mare and she was as ugly as anything you can imagine! But whenever he saw her he'd go crazy with passion even when she wasn't in season! She bred beautiful foals.' The mystery of Clavecimbel's attraction to the ugly mare remains unanswered, but after years of dressage experience Bert understands one truth: 'Genes do matter. Bloodlines prove themselves, they are so important. Talent is given by Nature.

'There are only a few top dressage horses, only a few can win Grand Prix. Expecting too much can ruin the rider-horse relationship, it is much better that the rider accepts the limitations of the horse. All horses can do the Grand Prix movements, but it is how they are going to learn and how they do the movements that separates the average horse from the star.'

Bert concentrates much of his energy training dressage horses and riders. 'I enjoy the training most, competition is the icing on the cake.' He can be classified as a caring, down-to-earth, warm-hearted guy and watching him you are spellbound. He has such a magic way with horses.

A diamond in the world of dressage, Bert's skills will continue to seep into the consciousness of many of the world's most discerning dressage riders.

LESSON FOUR · Training with Jane Bredin

For over seven years the Olympic rider Jane Bredin has been immersed in continental training methods, including five years as a student of Sjef Janssen. She

Jane Bredin

talks about her time spent living with a Dutch family: 'Being in that environment rubs off on you, you too start to think in a very professional way. No patchwork quilt ideas exist for the continentals. They give total commitment to dressage riding and pay special attention to the daily training programme. Because of this attitude the horse is disciplined into moving in a good way all the time. It is a lot fairer and means that the horse becomes more laid-back about competing because the rider is expecting nothing more than is being asked at home. The pressure is not always switched on, but everything is performed at one hundred per cent. For example, on a "bad" working day the horse is brought back to basics, but on a "good" day, new levels of excellence can be achieved – whatever the target, the concentration on excellence is total.'

In this section, Jane explains her interpretation of Sjef Janssen's dressage. Based on logic, innovation and knowledge, its viability is proven through successful competitors such as Anky van Grunsven and Jane Bredin herself. So what prompted Sjef to develop training methods quite different from other continentals? Jane explains, 'He wanted to train horses in a way in which improvement is perpetual. He wants everything smooth, a pleasant picture to watch, and the rider's aids subtle and light.' To make the principles easy to understand Jane has separated them into headings as follows:

1. Simplicity

2. Time-Factor

3. Training By Opposites

4. Submission

5. The Aids

6. The Working Movements

7. Fine Tuning

8. Muscle Power, Balance and Steady Connection

However, Jane points out that, in practice, the horse cannot be trained in isolated parts; the training fuses together from the beginning of the work through to the advanced stages.

SIMPLICITY

Simplicity lives at the core of this training. 'There must be no confusion; the horse must completely understand the rider's instructions. They are always applied the same way so the horse respects them and becomes responsive. The language between horse and rider is simplified. There are fewer mistakes through lack of understanding; the horse is less likely to spring surprises – he is confident in himself and the rider.'

By way of example, a student came to Jane with an Advanced horse, who had severe problems coping with the dressage work. Jane says, 'He had been off work for three years because of an injury, but previously he had been competing at Advanced level but always struggled. He has a good personality and is keen to please the rider and I believe he developed disobediences because he lacked understanding. This made him block against the rider in every way imaginable. To overcome his fears I schooled him in the basics because I wanted him to know how to respond to light leg and hand aids. Every time I applied an aid it was done in exactly the same manner. Steadily, it dawned on the horse how easy dressage really is and he stopped fighting me. He started muscling up over his top line, which helped him move forwards in a nice, round shape. He was developing self-carriage for the first time in his life. His confidence blossomed and so I taught advanced exercises and this time he found it all so easy! All because I'd kept the instructions simple. You could almost hear him sighing with relief.'

TIME-FACTOR

'Time is paramount to good training. Never train to a time limit because it results in cutting corners and impacts on the final quality. Approach every single part of the horse's training with a long-term view. There are no excuses, no "perhaps if I tweaked this or that!" There are no quick fixes, there is only the reality of working to get it right. DO NOT CUT CORNERS! AT YOUR PERIL! Train the horse according to his capabilities. This varies with each stage of his education. Think of every horse as an individual. Adhering to rigid training schedules stifles individuality and courts disaster. Be ready to progress. Never lose sight of perfecting the basics and the feel the horse is giving you.

'With the time-factor you have to be flexible. An example of this is a very extravagant-moving horse. His hind legs were so active he physically could not stop the forward momentum of his back-end almost overtaking his front-end and this made him panic. Teaching him to cope with his extravagant action took a long time, and to achieve it, I had to nurture his confidence so he learnt to manage his way of going in a more reserved style.

'The time spent training in each session can fluctuate. For example, one day a horse may need one hour's schooling, and another day he may need fifteen minutes. Taking this concept further, some horses take a year (or even longer) to consolidate the working gaits and others may take six months (or even less, but this is unusual). The horse is trained at the rate he learns, and at every stage of this learning, his level of understanding must be total. This approach coaches the horse's physical and psychological fitness; it prepares him for the demands of the work without him even realising it is difficult! The rider has remained flexible to the needs of the horse, but at the same time, developed him along a structured training programme.'

Training for Competition

'Novice classes are designed for inexperienced riders or young horses, and to encourage not discourage. It is no sin to educate the horse in competitions. For example, if a young horse became wobbly up the centre line, or was mischevious, or broke from the canter, he should not be harshly marked by the judge. Young Horse classes judge the way of going; they are less precise than specific tests and make competition more enjoyable and easier for the horse. They promote good training. All Novice tests offer opportunities to boost the confidence of rider and horse and they should be ridden with these healthy attitudes.

'At Elementary level the work becomes more difficult, the foundations for the collected and extended gaits are being laid (simple changes, 10m circles and medium trot) and it is no longer acceptable, for example, just to show lengthened strides, now the horse must go in medium trot from marker to marker. The allowances given to the Novice horse no longer exist; from Elementary level upwards the horse is expected to show athleticism and a way of going that hallmarks dressage.

'Realistically, it takes the everyday rider three years to step from Novice to Advanced Medium competition, whereas the experienced rider might take half this time. The horse's temperament must be considered, for example a hot character may take longer to settle to the flying changes. He might need to stay at Medium level longer than a steadier horse before he upgrades to Advanced Medium competition. The rider plays the rules to suit the horse and never the other way around!'

TRAINING BY OPPOSITES

'With the novice horse, training by opposites is black and white. The rider assesses the natural deficiencies of the horse and trains in the opposite way. For example, if the horse rushes, he is ridden forwards more slowly; one who is slow or lazy is ridden more briskly forwards; a horse with a naturally high head carriage is ridden with more roundness through his back, whereas one with a naturally lower head carriage is ridden slightly more "up".

'A good example of this is a talented horse I own, who is an introverted character. He is active but his rhythm rushes and he holds his breath whenever I ask for anything new because he is nervous and lacks confidence. My aim was to encourage him to have a more bold and constructive attitude to his work. I applied the principle of training by opposites and asked him for less energy so that he moved slower than he naturally wanted to go. Gradually, he adopted this trained "way of going" as if he were born to it. Now his nervousness has dissipated and I can ride him up to his talents.

'Another example is a stallion with a big, springy trot. I could not contain his trot, it was just too extravagant! I asked him to work in a shorter trot that is neater and more contained. I knew that once he became settled into this new rhythm he would automatically have the extra power to develop a good working trot (which would later develop into a medium and extended trot). The primary training for the working, collected, medium and extended trot was to train the horse in the opposite way from which he would naturally move.

'Working by opposites can progress movements through learning curves. The rider puts the horse into a position where he starts a movement and, if he gets into any difficulties, finds an easier way to overcome them and only returns to the exercise when the horse feels comfortable with it and can cope with it completely. The rider then repeats the exercise to consolidate it. The horse has been *allowed* to cope mentally – what he may originally have considered a difficult exercise has become easy. For example, if the horse is struggling in the working pirouettes, put him in shoulder-in position, reset the balance and then restart the working pirouettes. The horse does not actually know he is doing this difficult exercise because the rider merely suggests it quietly and simply. The rider has the ultimate brain and uses this asset to help the horse but without putting him under pressure.

'It is obvious that if a horse runs you slow him down and if he is too slow you speed him up, but when he has a problem through the body the rider can only reduce it by degrees. In effect, the rider manipulates the horse without presenting him with difficulties. Life is made easy for him, so he wants to learn and oblige the rider. For example, say the horse is stiff on his right side, ride left shoulder-in which flexes him to the left and then ask him into right renvers so that he flexes and loosens himself to the right . The rider is always working to reduce a problem. For the more advanced horse training by opposites evolves into training by degrees. A classic example is teaching the medium trot. People often go to a trainer and say, "My horse is not capable of doing medium trot, what should I do?" In this scenario the trainer would suggest, "Instead of trying to go the whole of the arena in medium trot go just a few steps, return to collected trot and then repeat medium trot." The horse learns to be confident, he is not being over-pushed. Gradually his balance improves and he can cope with more and more medium trot until he can go across the diagonal without losing rhythm or balance. This can only be trained by degrees.'

SUBMISSION

In dressage, submission is the ultimate joining of forces – the beauty of the horse's movement married with the intelligence and compassion of the rider. The horse accepts the bridle, goes to meet the bridle and takes no opportunities to resist or rebel – all the benefits of lightness and balance slot gracefully into place. In competition, submission is explained as '*attention and confidence, harmony, lightness and ease of the movements, acceptance of the bridle and lightness of the forehand.*

'In this method submission is taught without impulsion. Many horses become "lighter" when you add momentum, but without realising it the rider's hands are moving. Nine times out of ten the horse is not submissive the moment you ask for more than halt or walk – he goes forwards and the energy zips out the front end. Many riders believe that if they tweak the rein and soften quickly the horse responds by becoming lighter on the rein. In truth, the horse is light because there's no rein pressure and not because the horse accept the bit!

'In submission, it is important that the horse is happy to be on the bit and is "soft" on the rein and when he understands submission at halt and walk, he can be taught it in trot and canter. For a young horse, this could be walk and trot on a circle.'

Self-carriage in a young horse

The Submission Point

Jane explains how to teach submission. 'Firstly, the horse has to understand the submission point. To achieve this the rider takes up the reins to a point where it is possible to get the horse to "give" with a steady restraint until he softens to the rein. The rider holds the restraint until the horse softens. This is the submission point.

'The time factor is crucial to the success of submission because you cannot rush it. *Start with a small degree*; a millimetre, an inch, then three inches, then gradually you build on it. Horses throw up different reactions: some oblige immediately and say, "Okay, that's easy". Others resist, step backwards or rock or stand with their forelegs straight out in front of them in a peculiar way. Some hollow their backs or hunch their backs, some shut their eyes and nibble themselves. The rider must be patient. If the horse has a problem do not speed up the process, he has to figure out his own submission point. This is the key to submission. If the horse has a strong character and likes to pit his athleticism against the rider (which can some-times happen, particularly with stallions and mares) as a safety net and a way to help the horse so that he understands what I want more easily, I use draw reins. It is much better that the horse learns the right way, otherwise the wrong reaction can easily become a bad habit. Be warned: *draw reins must never be used to pull the horse's head "in", or as a restraint, or to put pressure on the horse's mouth.* NEVER!! Hold the draw reins comfortably so the horse is reminded not to challenge the rider; they act as a barrier beyond which the horse cannot go – never in any way do they exert force.

'Never, never take a horse on in the mouth. Never pull back. Give the horse time to understand your requests. Build up a little more understanding, a little more submission each day, a little bit more tomorrow, and so on. Know that once the penny has dropped, once the horse has figured out the release point, he will submit willingly, find his balance and learn not to lean on the rider's hands and use them as a prop. The horse learns to understand that if he gives to the rider he automatically rewards himself by a softer feel coming on the rein. If you cheat by fiddling with the reins you can improve the contact for a fleeting second, but as soon as you retake the contact the horse leans on your hands again. You are back where you started and will probably have to begin the whole tweaking business again! So you can see that, by allowing the horse to know his own submission point, he finds the degree of rein contact acceptable and he will not take liberties with this degree of contact because he has decided on it himself. The rider has shown him the path towards this softness, not by fiddling with the hands but by keeping the contact steady. Of course, as the horse's balance progresses he comes lighter on the bridle, but never is the rider constantly nagging him, tweaking and pulling on the rein in a vain effort to get this lightness, I cannot repeat this often enough – STEADY CONTACT, LIGHT HANDS.'

Equal Pressure on Both Reins

'The reins are held so there is an equal pressure on both sides of the horse's mouth. If he gives an uneven feel in the mouth, the rider taking a stronger contact on his stiffer side will not improve his acceptance of the contact. For example, if he is lighter on the left rein and heavier on the right rein the rider keeps the connection steady on both sides because if not, if the contact is given on the heavier side, or the horse is bent that way to loosen him off, the left contact hand becomes ineffective. The horse may give on his heavier side (stiff side) and become lighter, but in reality he is still not accepting the bit on the side that feels lighter (the hollow side). So, when the rider stops bending him and the horse straightens his head and neck in front of his shoulders, the contact will still not be equal – the rider has achieved nothing. This is where many people go wrong. They try and make the horse "give in" on his stiff side but what is needed is for him to accept the contact on the hollow side and then he comes less stiff on the stiff side. The rider is aiming to equalise the connection by taking an equal contact on both reins and riding the horse into that contact.

'If a horse comes and goes inconsistently on the contact, which can happen, for example, in a movement where he stiffens and grabs the bit, keep the hands still. If you have done your homework and the horse understands the rein effects he will come to the bit. Most importantly, if a horse cannot accept the bit when you are just walking and halting he certainly will not be able to accept it in the movements.'

Riding the Horse in a Round Shape

'The horse is worked in a round shape until he becomes strong through his shoulders, balanced and well-muscled through his back. The young horse is trained most of the time in this round shape and may be ridden in a higher head carriage for a brief period of time, for example five to ten minutes per training session.

'The amount of time the young horse is capable of holding this higher head carriage is achieved as a result of him working correctly through his top line. Never by the rider pulling on the reins to bring the horse's head up. The advanced

Showing light
head carriage

horse is trained with a higher head carriage for longer periods of time but this
work is sandwiched in between times when he is ridden "rounder". This checks
he is working through his back. Only ride the horse with a higher head carriage
for as long as he can stay light in the hand and supple in the back, neck and jaw.
The moment there is any lack of balance or stiffness, return to the "round" way of
going, and return to the higher head carriage when that top quality way of going
is re-established.

'Once the suppleness and "throughness" are established, the horse will find it easy to keep his self-carriage and show this higher head carriage in all its glory – he will feel wonderfully light, expressive and free in his gaits. To clarify, submission is acceptance of the bit and for this to be achievable the horse must willingly want to submit.'

General Information on Submission

'As explained, this form of submission asks the horse to come "round" because it supples and stretches the muscles over his top line, at the same time as training him to follow the hand. I do not ride all horses this deep all the time. Each horse is an individual and I tailor the training to match his needs.

'This submission differs from many continental training methods. Many favour "long and low". This is where the horse stretches his head and neck right down by his knees and even lower. "Long and low" stretches the top line muscles but to a lesser degree of submission, and to perform the movements the horse has to raise his head and neck. However, with the "round and deep" submission the horse can do the movements because the roundness comes from the horse being "up and in" rather than "long and low". Riding them in this "round" way never detracts from the horse's balance, but with the "long and low" method, unless a horse is built naturally "uphill" and has powerful hind legs there is a danger of putting him on his forehand.'

Flexing

Flexing prepares and teaches the beginnings of independent bend. 'There's no exaggerated bend, just an inclination. I start flexing the young horse just a little (¼–½in), particularly on the stiff side. I am asking him to loosen behind the poll. I ride with my hands held wide apart and sympathetic. Initially, I only flex him for short periods. I introduce it on circles, then straight lines and, as he becomes more supple, in the lateral work, that is, leg-yield and three-track shoulder-in.

'With the more developed horse I have established straightness, and then I develop bend. This starts to happen automatically from the lateral work and as the horse advances I expect much more of an "uphill" inside bend. The feeling in the hand is the same tension, but the horse comes lighter on the inside rein through engagement of his inside hind leg.

'In order to bend, the horse has to be able to stretch the outside of his body more than the inside. If you do not allow inside bend the rider is forcing the horse onto the outside rein and forcing the bend in the neck – obviously this is totally wrong for good dressage. By teaching flexing as a softening exercise and integrating it into the early training, and then developing it as the straightness improves, the horse learns to follow the hand.'

Bending

This form of bending is different from flexing and is used as a suppling, loosening exercise. The horse is asked for a good, healthy degree of bend to the inside; he becomes lighter on the inside and more connected on the outside rein. Bending increases his ability to remain straight on turns, circles and straight lines. Jane warns *It should only be used with discretion and only be taught at the appropriate time and in the appropriate way.* Establish submission, lightness from the leg and straightness before starting bending because if the horse is not submissive he will flick his head from side to side, his shoulders will fall out and he will become unbalanced. Basically, in this situation, the horse lacks straightness and to compensate for this he evades the exercise. These are the reasons why bending must be used discreetly and at the right time of the horse's training.

'Never pull at the horse and force him to bend. Initially, trot him on a circle in a deep outline and ask him to loosen off the inside rein. Think of keeping the quarters to the bend. Once he can perform bending on a circle well you can introduce it on straight lines.'

THE AIDS

Light off the Legs

'The rider's legs hang loosely down the sides of the horse and are positioned slightly in front of the girth. The leg is "off" when hanging in a natural, loose way (the leg is never used in a gripping action). The rider uses the leg in "on" mode with one small indication of what is needed, in the same forward position. The rider aims for the tiniest reaction from the leg. Do not continually touch the horse with your legs because this produces more energy than needed and makes him resistant in the mouth. Only use the leg when needed because if he is "up" to the bridle he will go forward to the bit on his own. Light leg aids become elevated into even lighter signals until they are mere whispers to the horse.'

[*James Fillis, the distinguished rider of the nineteenth century, also used this leg position. He was renowned as a great dressage artist and trained a great number of horses. He had an influence on French and Russian dressage.*]

Jane explains, 'If the horse is lazy off my leg, and working "round" in my hand, I will speed up the trot so that he understands that I want more forwardness. Once he is moving very forwards I will slow the trot down to the tempo that suits him. With a horse who is really dead to my legs, I would prod him with my heels at the same time as dropping the contact (this double-checks that I am not blocking his desire to move promptly forwards). Immediately he responds I return to using the lightest of leg aids.

'The rider helps the horse by finding the speed in each gait (walk, trot and canter) that suits the individual horse. This speed, this "gear" is discovered by observing how the horse moves naturally.' (See section on Training By Opposites.)

'Normally, we do not use whips because they usually make the horse quick off the whip aids rather than quick off the leg aids. There are exceptions to this rule, for example, when first teaching the canter pirouettes. The whip is only ever applied as a "booster aid" and NEVER as a punishment. The rider uses the voice if an inexperienced horse needs more forwardness, or steadying down. The horse's quick reactions to the leg are preserved by the rider always finding ways to ask for forwardness by lighter and lighter indications.'

The Hands

'The rider's hands act as an anchor – not fixed but more as a restraint.' Jane explains further: 'If your hands are held low near the horse's neck you can keep them motionless, but the moment they are raised higher they move. Obviously, the amount of movement depends on the experience of the rider – however the pure physics governing the laws of Nature says they do jolt up and down. Still hands are best for the horse.

'By holding the hands to the horse's withers the rider maintains a consistent, light connection with the horse's mouth. In the collected work the classical line (from the rider's elbow, wrist and hands to the horse's mouth) is kept because the horse elevates his forehand. The snaffle reins are normally held under the little fingers and, with the double bridle, the curb reins are held under the third fingers and the snaffle reins under the little fingers. This ensures that most of the pressure is on the bradoon and not the curb bit. When the horse has progressed into an advanced outline he is schooled in the double bridle and will only be ridden in a snaffle when hacked out or lunged. This is common practice on the continent, the thinking being if a horse is hardly ridden in a double how can he learn to accept the feel of it? When you start using the double bridle follow two principles; first, take the horse back to very basic work and second, only ride more advanced exercises when the horse happily accepts the double bridle in the basic work.

'Check that the double bridle fits correctly. Generally, I use a French fixed curb of standard thickness. This curb does not have a port but is slightly raised in the middle to give room for the horse's tongue. The bradoon can be French link or single-jointed.' Jane is obsessed with the correct fitting of the double bridle: 'The horse must be comfortable in his mouth. The bridle, especially the cavesson and the bits must fit correctly. The horse should have his teeth checked by a good dentist approximately every six months.'

The Seat

'Never sit against the horse. Sit light. Never overdrive with the seat because this will start a battle between the horse's front and back ends. Sometimes, with an advanced horse, the rider sits more deliberately for a moment, that is, sits a little deeper and then lightens the seat – for example in piaffe and passage, medium, extended trot and the canter pirouettes. I would advise getting the help of a professional trainer if you have any doubts as to how and when the back should be applied. The golden rules are: *never strong, never heavy.*'

The Half-Halts

'To execute a half-halt correctly, a horse has to be very balanced. We train the half-halts in a gradual build-up way because they are such a precise thing to ride. Sometimes even good riders get the timing wrong. Teach the half-halts when the horse understands rein pressure. Badly ridden half-halts do the opposite of what is wanted, they unbalance the horse. If a rider half-halts a young horse who is not working through his back, his forward momentum is checked for a split second, but instead of the energy returning to the hindquarters and enhancing elevation what actually happens is that his balance comes more onto the forehand. The absolute beginning of half-halting is using prompt-reacting transitions from trot/walk/trot. Once the reactions become quicker and lighter, progress to trot half-halts. A good way to introduce the half-halts is by asking the horse to wait, to slow down, for example just before a corner.' (See also Riding Corners and Turns.) 'Think slow yourself, do not pull on the horse's mouth, and let the horse stay in balance! Conrad Schumacher explains it well: "Drive in, take back, drive out." Obviously, the "driving" is light.

'With an advanced horse the half-halt is a refined way of riding. For example, provided the horse is moving forwards I do not use my leg aids, I ask for the half-halt through the balance of sitting and waiting for that moment of restraint of the forward movement coming through the shoulders, and then apply the half-halt more through a deepening of my seat, but making sure the horse feels soft through his back. Then I allow the horse to move forwards and at this time I might, if necessary, put my legs on. My half-halt takes a *moment of movement* and balances it. Carefully, I nurture and preserve the forward movement, always allowing the natural spring of the horse to step through.'

THE WORKING MOVEMENTS

'Working movements identify which parts of a movement need improvement. They supple and strengthen the horse. They prepare him for the full movement without demanding too much from him psychologically or physically. They promote quality of dressage because the horse is trained "to" a movement and he is only ridden in the full movement when he can go well in the working exercises. Working movements are the "babies", the building blocks of the adult ones. They are the homework, the preparation that breaks down each full movement into its component parts. This makes learning easier for the horse and boosts his confidence in the rider. To explain further, an introverted type of horse may need more psychological support. He asks the rider, "What do you want me to do next?" The rider must give clear messages to such a horse, and be patient, and not ask too much too soon and be sure the horse understands before progressing. Horses are generous creatures, instead of disobeying an impatient rider they are likely to try to please, but because they are physically undeveloped they just tighten and perform the movement badly. The rider must wait until every part of the working exercises can be controlled, then piece them together to form the full movement. If the horse needs strengthening up or has a bad day, return to the working movements.'

Corners and Circles

Corners are one of the testaments to the genius of this training method. You see young horses canter deep into corners keeping the rhythm, keeping the balance. They remain upright on all four legs (that is, they do not become unbalanced or lose straightness by throwing their quarters and/or shoulders in or out of the turn). 'The rider approaches the corner in a gait which is sufficiently forwards. Do not slow the horse down if he is behind the leg. If he is in front of the leg, think "slow" in your mind. Approaching the corner in this steady tempo gives the horse the chance to keep his balance, and keeping this balance through corners is essential to developing better engagement and straightness. The rider makes a conscious effort to hold the rhythm in the seat whilst the horse steps through. This work adds muscle power and self-carriage to the horse's way of going.

'To ride a corner approach it square to the turn. Let the outside rein follow the horse's bend in his neck so he has the freedom to make a smooth turn and slide the inside leg slightly forwards of the girth, this stops the shoulder cutting in. Give the horse time to come round your inside leg and come out of the corner continuing in the same gait. The outside leg is placed wherever it is needed, for example at the exit of the corner forwards of the girth for more impulsion, or behind the girth if the quarters swing out.

'Riding a circle is similar to riding a corner and the rider uses the aids in a similar way. To avoid a common pitfall be vigilant to keep your horse parallel through his body. He must maintain the circular shape the whole way round and his hind legs should follow the same line as the forelegs.'

Working Shoulder-In

'If the horse is in front of the leg I begin training shoulder-in along the long side of the arena and I do this by simply asking him to come looser on the inside rein. This improves inside bend, and at the same time, the horse learns that it is easy to move his body in one direction and look in another. When he has the confidence to be light on the inside bend (and not hold onto it for balance) then his shoulders are positioned to the inside of the track for shoulder-in.' Untrained horses bend their heads and necks easily to one side and more stiffly to the other. 'I'll do a little shoulder-in on a circle with a young horse, or even just ask him to move off my inside leg. These techniques encourage him to offer shoulder-in bend quite naturally. You can start to make them supple quite early on.

'The young horse needs more space while learning shoulder-in and the rider must be able to open or shut the angle to help him maintain balance. For this reason, and also because if the horse wobbles to the left or right he might clatter the arena boards and scare himself, I sometimes teach shoulder-in down the centre line. If the horse moves behind the centre line I ride him forwards to it, but if he moves over it I ride him so he comes back to it. This way he learns not to be nervous and the rider learns to have more control over the exactness of the shoulder-in movement.

Early stages of introducing a young horse to the idea of shoulder-in

Three-track shoulder-in for a young horse

'On the rein to which the horse bends easily, and if he is not moving actively forwards, I will ride him in leg-yield, keeping his head and neck fairly straight, and ask for plenty of energy. On the stiff side I will add inside bend and ride shoulder-in. Initially, I ask for a few strides of whatever angle or bend I am schooling and I only increase this number of strides when the horse responds to my aids, remaining balanced and in good rhythm. You have to ride the young horse as he reacts each day. For example, one day he may give four good strides of shoulder-in, the next ten. Gradually he will grow in strength and perform correct three-track shoulder-in showing an equal degree of bend to both sides of his body.'

Working Travers

'The first stage of teaching the horse travers is training him to leg-yield. He must understand moving sideways from the leg then, once this is established, ask him to leg-yield his quarters off the track (for example, if on the left rein, the rider's right leg instructs the horse to yield the left side of his body off the track so that his quarters move on a separate track from his forehand). This is a good way to introduce the really green horse to travers. Make sure you hold the front end straight. Once he can give left bend ask him to yield from the right leg, then change the bend from left to right so he is looking down the arena track – now he is correct for travers. Like all the other working movements, gradually introduce more difficult aspects when the horse can handle them. The travers begins teaching the horse to bend through his ribcage and this is a crucial step in preparing him for the more difficult demands of the half-pass.'

Introducing a young horse to the idea of travers, showing little bend

Working Half-Pass

'The working half-pass is very progressive – a little angle, shoulder forward and the horse learns to go independently off the inside rein. Ride the horse along the track in shoulder-in position and then take a few steps to the inside of the track, and then ride straight again and repeat the exercise. Keep the horse straight in his body but with an independent flexion; when you can control the straightness of the horse it is easy to ask him to come soft on the rein and add a little bend through the body. Control the shoulder with the outside rein and use the outside leg (but never too strongly) to ask the horse to cross over his legs. The inside leg stops his shoulders falling in, keeps the bend and the forwardness.

Observe the rider's leg and hand position for half-pass

'As the working half-passes improve, the true half-passes can be ridden. The preparatory exercises are shoulder-in, travers, renvers. Initially for half-pass my language is think forwards trot, think shoulder-fore and travers position with the horse's body. The aids, if anything, are a bit more weight on the inside seat-bone and a trot "uphill". All good half-passes are ridden very forward-thinking.

'But I always start the rider with travers across the whole diagonal of the school before I even begin half-pass. When the horse, and the student, are ready for the half-passes they do not ride exactly marker to marker because if the horse is set up wrong it destroys them; the rider has a bad feeling and the horse learns a bad feeling. To begin working half-pass on the left rein for example, trot up the centre line, do not start the half-pass until the horse is listening, wait until he takes the left bend, shoulder-fore and then ride half-pass position to the track. The rider will end up in the chosen direction if the horse's shoulders are pointed in that direction.

'The half-pass is proper bend forwards, that is to say, the shoulder stays pretty straight, the bend is in the ribcage and the hind legs cross over so the horse moves on parallel lines. The moment the rider takes the half-pass too steep too soon, the horse loses rhythm and balance. He falls onto his inside or outside shoulder, leads with his hindquarters or leaves them trailing and in this unbalanced way of going he finds it impossible to trot in a clean rhythm. As in all the movements, the quality of the basic way of going is essential. It is the same with level contact, if the horse does not take an equal rein contact on the left and right side of the bit the left and right half-passes can never be equally good.

'If I said to an experienced rider, 'Come out of the corner, position the shoulders to B and then ride travers, they would ride an angle that looks like an advanced half-pass. In all the training, from Novice to Grand Prix, everything is about having the shoulders free. If the horse is not supple, the rider trains the horse's shoulders to be in advance of his body and then the quarters follow. The moment the quarters overtake the tiniest bit it destroys the forwardness. So the rules are: until the horse is quite developed and the rider can control the position of his shoulders it is best to keep the half-passes very forward-going with little angle.'

Working Pirouettes

Physically and mentally these prepare the horse for the demands of the full pirouettes. Jane says: 'The rider must know precisely the right time to teach the working pirouettes.' Below is a guideline:

1. When the horse has fully learned all the lateral work in walk, trot and canter, the working walk pirouettes can be started.

2. The working canter pirouettes can be taught once the horse can collect the canter and perform all lateral work in walk, trot and canter.

In the working canter pirouettes the horse steps on two parallel circles, that is his hind feet move on a smaller circle than his forefeet. Initially, the larger circle is 20m, so that the 'smaller' circle is only fractionally less than 20m, and at first it is performed in walk, then trot and finally canter. To make those first steps of teaching the working pirouettes easy the rider takes the working travers straight along the arena walls and then top-and-tails the ends of these straight travers lines with two half-moon shapes. These are ridden like two parallel circular lines similar to that of the working pirouette. The horse progresses from this simplified exercise to the proper version of the working pirouettes. The rider knows when the horse is proficient at these when he can maintain the accuracy of the two parallel circles, and at the same time keep the steps of the canter of equal measured lengthss. The rider continues with this exercise until the horse performs it well every time it is ridden. The strength and stamina of the horse builds up. The rider should feel that, if the horse were asked for a smaller working pirouette, he would respond willingly and without losing balance. At this time, the two parallel circles can be slightly reduced in size. Gradually, the horse performs the working pirouettes on smaller and smaller parallel circles until the circles get so small they evolve into true canter pirouettes. The emphasis must be that the horse finds all these exercises easy and consistently maintains balance and rhythm. Canter pirouettes are one of the most difficult dressage movements.

'To explain the aids for the working pirouette: we take both hands to the outside and the rider's weight is a tiny bit more emphasised towards the outside. The inside hand goes almost to the top of the wither. In theory we hold the shoulder out, and once the horse can maintain the correct bend to the inside, we allow the quarters in, but it is not the same as travers. The rider's inside leg is

Working pirouette

applied lightly and rests forward on the girth to stop the shoulder turning too quickly. The outside leg is held fractionally behind the girth and again is only applied lightly. By riding these two parallel circles the rider is learning the skills that enhance canter pirouette riding abilities. For example:

1. The rider can control the exact degree to which the horse is allowed to turn.

2. The rider can place the hindquarters precisely where required.

3. The amount of inside bend can be regulated.

4. The canter can be fine-tuned into measured, equal steps.

5. The rider can alter the degree of collection to suit the needs of the horse at any particular stage of his training in this movement.'

'To explain further: start the movement with shoulder-fore, position the shoulders very slightly to the inside of the larger parallel circle (the bend is towards the inside into the shoulder-fore), then ask the horse to bring his quarters onto a smaller parallel circle. These working pirouettes clarify the weaknesses and strengths of the horse's balance. For example: Are the quarters coming across too much to the inside of the circle? Are the shoulders stiff? Is the bend too much, too little or correct? The rider can quickly identify which areas of the exercise the horse finds difficult and concentrate on those weaknesses. The rider knows when something is wrong with the horse's balance because if there is a break somewhere, it is not correct, and the interruption can be felt and corrected. However, when it is correct the whole movement flows and seems very natural to the horse. Practising canter pirouettes too often as a finished movement can put too much pressure on the horse and does not necessarily improve his abilities in this difficult movement. The working pirouettes "set up" and prepare him for their demands.'

Working Flying Changes

Some young horses are naturally well balanced in the canter and so introducing the first single flying changes can be constructive. 'With the young horse it is more of a change of direction than a flying change. Typically, we would ask for this "change of direction" at the end of the short diagonal. It is important that the horse continues in the same rhythm of the canter before, during and after this "change of direction" and shows no tension or nervousness.

'As the horse progresses and accepts, without fear or anxiety, the flying changes of direction, the rider can start to be more explicit with the aids: the rider sits in balance to collected canter and asks the horse to make the single flying change by moving the new outside leg behind the girth and sliding the new inside leg forward. The seat slides into the rhythm of the change in a fluid and easy way.

Flying changes on a young horse

These simple aids (which the horse must be responsive to, and comfortable with) lend themselves well to teaching the sequence changes.

'The horse is ready to learn the one-time flying changes when he is relaxed and competent about all the canter change work from the single to the two-time flying changes. In the one-time changes, the rider's legs swing in the rhythm of what the one-time flying changes should be, and so the horse understands that he should jump from one leading leg to the other.'

Piaffe and Passage

This is where experience counts because there are no real hard-and-fast rules about piaffe and passage. 'A rider who gets into trouble with these movements should not play around with them, but should get help from a professional trainer. Piaffe and passage are not difficult for the horse, but a rider who has limited talent or is inexperienced will create problems by training incorrectly. If the horse offers either the piaffe or passage naturally and the rider understands the principles, there is no harm in doing a few half-steps, but always without any ultimate stress factor so the horse learns them as simply different "gears".

'At prize-givings we joke about the piaffe and passage because if a horse comes out on his toes and offers either movement you have a hope he will learn them

Piaffe

easily and this is obviously exciting for the trainer. But generally we do not teach piaffe or passage too early because some horses use them against you, for example coming into a walk pirouette in a competition. The rider must select the right time to teach them. Some horses learn them early because they find them so easy, but often these horses are the type that should only practise them a little and be reintroduced to them later in their training. Other horses start them later and may need to be taught them every day, but have the temperament and the strength to take the discipline. Piaffe and passage require rider tact, sensitivity and experience and once taught they add extra dimensions to energy, spring and cadence.'

Fine-Tuning

To achieve 100 per cent better results there will be periods of drafting and redrafting of the basics. 'I go over the same ground, ask for a touch more refinement, a touch more lightness from the leg, a touch more softness in the hand. With a young horse who is starting something new, I do not rush him, I work on more balance, more in front of the leg, more submission, more collection, better transitions. I repeat it continually until they get better and better.'

MUSCLE POWER, CONNECTION AND BALANCE

The dressage rider's finest reward is the consolidation of the horse's balance. It develops progressively through the beginning, middle and advanced stages of training. Balance is the dividend paid for all the time, skills and techniques invested by the rider. Balance acts as a barometer of schooling efficiency. It transforms the ordinary horse into a graceful dancer.

But what is the formula for getting this balance? How and where does it come from? Jane explains, 'At first you may get only glimpses. A youngster's balance in the working gaits obviously differs from that of an advanced horse in the collected or extended gaits. Train the horse at the level of balance he can give at each stage of his training and the balance will germinate. He becomes smoother and more pleasant to watch; he comes to attention throughout his body. He holds himself more elegantly. His shoulders are free, more weight comes onto the hind legs and he feels wonderful and light to ride.

'The developed muscles hold the horse connected in his balance for longer periods and he is trained to that steady connection. A youngster lacks it, but as the dressage horse is improved by his developed strength, and his submission improves, he gains the ultimate form of contained energy. With this, the hind legs can push, the push goes to the rider's hand and the horse stays consistently on the bit.' But Jane warns, 'If the push is more than the horse can hold, the energy will go out the front door (or he will put his head up too high, or too low, or come onto his forehand or splay his hindquarters out behind him). However, if he stays up to the end of the rein more push means more power, more elasticity, more elevation – muscle power equals steady connection, and this equals good balance.'

SUMMARY

The rider is continually working to improve the horse and his level of training. The key points of this training method are:

1. The horse is taught in a simple and consistent way with good communication. This is the most effective and compassionate way of training.

2. Working in harmony with the horse creates good dressage and avoids confusion.

3. Impulsion is inextricably linked to the horse being in front of the leg.

4. Submission is taught as a priority and improved continually.

5. The rider is always refining the basics: more lightness, more acceptance of the bit, more self-carriage.

6. The horses are trained according to their individual needs: only when a horse feels comfortable are new exercises taught.

7. Nothing is taught through force, only through muscle power, steady connection and balance.

JANE BREDIN'S PROFILE

She's an Amazon of a girl with the guts to take life's knocks and carry on regardless, always reaching out to fly towards her zenith, with a dream she has believed in since the early 1980s.

Making dreams come true takes tornadoes of ambition and a tigerish determination. Add exceptional talent, a touch of genius and you might – just might – make it happen. Jane's dream is to win medals.

Her good fortune in dressage started when she began training with David Hunt. Soon she was working for him, and spent eleven years as his head girl. This period embedded knowledge into Jane's skills: she rode many different types of horses and these experiences built up an enormous library of 'feels'. She travelled with David as his groom to many international shows and watched some of the 'greats' such as Klimke and Rehbein. Jane was surprised: 'I saw a lot of good riding, but I also saw riders making mistakes, and that made me realise that becoming an international dressage rider was achievable.' Fired with ambition, she traded in her yellow Renault for a chestnut horse! This 'swapsie' acquired her first dressage horse, Bertie Wooster. She laughs, 'That car was my pride and joy, but of course I have no regrets. He was a wonderful horse.' In her first international competition in Spain in 1987, Jane rode Bertie with fellow riders Sarah Dwyer-Coles and Louise Francis. 'It was great fun, we made some friends and won enough prize money to pay our way.' Working twelve hours a day, every day, and teaching to supplement her income, Jane was making her dream happen – she was given the ride on Soldier Boy, a Thoroughbred owned by a client of David Hunt, and it was this horse who gave Jane her first international placing of 7th in an Intermediaire I small tour competition.

By 1991, with the help of her aunt, Sheila Duvollet, Jane bought a potential top international horse who was working at Prix St Georges level. Sadly, six months later, Verdi went lame and after two years of continuous treatments it was decided to retire him to grass. 'I can remember going to the Barcelona Olympics and watching and crying thinking about Verdi, but in a way it made me even more determined to make it. I so wanted to compete at the Olympics.'

In 1992 Jane and Susie Cumine moved to Sandpits Farm, near Corsham in Wiltshire. Originally a pig farm, it took the imagination of Susie's husband Anthony to transform the place into an attractive stable complex. Sandpits Farm has a pleasant family atmosphere; students come to Jane for lessons and Susie and Jane both help to run the yard. As with any great performance, the quality of the support team plays an integral part in the end results and this is certainly true of Jane's success in national and international competitions. The unstinting support leaves her free to concentrate on riding every inch of every dressage test and this focused concentration is very much Jane's style.

Born an optimist, after Verdi's lameness and all the sorrows that went with it, Jane waited. By 1993 she began to realise there was a superstar right in the yard and right under her nose, Affectionately known as 'Dido', Cupido is a great one for polo mints. 'He revels in the VIP treatment; he thinks of himself as a very superior horse.' Owned by Susie, Jane took over the ride once Cupido started competing at Medium Level. 'The first time I ever rode him in a test, I thought, "This is a dressage horse."'

Jane on a fun day out with her friend and business partner, Susie Cumine: pairs dressage at a charity event

Jane Bredin riding Cupido at the 1996 Olympic Games

'This horse loves pressure. The more pressure the better he likes it. When he works, he works and when he rests, he rests, there is no in between with him.' Cupido saves every drop of his strength to zap out his brilliance in the arena. Jane explains his progress: 'He has not been straightforward to train. He wants to please and he finds everything so easy, but he has such power: sometimes it goes over the top. For example, in his early days, in his extended trot his hind legs used to thrust forwards so vigorously that he would unbalance himself and drop onto his fore-hand, pitching onto your hands.' Jane joined forces with international trainer Sjef Janssen in 1994. 'He took us back to basics. Walk to halt, halt to walk, transitions and more transitions, trot to walk. Cupido had to be soft and drop onto the contact and be forward from the leg. We did no dressage movements that first winter of training with Sjef. Nothing more than basics. I spent hours riding Cupido in halt to walk. I was beginning to think I couldn't even ride a 20m circle.'

But the hard work began to pay. Cupido began to give outstanding performances: in 1995 he was 3rd in the s'Hertogenbosch Grand Prix and 3rd in the Intermediaire II; 4th in the Bercy CDI-W Grand Prix and 5th in the Kür; 2nd in the Warsaw CEI Grand Prix Kür and the Grand Prix; 2nd in the Pamfou CDI Grand Prix; 1st in the Hickstead CDI Grand Prix and the Grand Prix Special. All these successes resulted in Jane being selected with Cupido for the 1996 Atlanta Olympic Games. 'But I was disappointed with our performance at the Games. We really were not on our usual good form.'

Fresh back from Atlanta and still burning with the ambition to win, Jane had time to think long and hard. 1998 brought her the salvation she had been looking for. There was no more need to take the long and exhausting training trips over to the continent. She says, 'British dressage has a new approach to its top riders. They asked all the team riders if they would agree to train consistently with Conrad Schumacher, and of course this has given us all excellent training. This input is helping us as competitors and as trainers of the future.'

Jane has four horses to compete now, not least among them Goya, who is new to Prix St Georges competition and shows a breathtaking piaffe and passage. There is also Lucky Star, who came 5th in the Shearwater 6 Year Old Championships. 'Fate always dictates, and there is always a reason for everything.' In her typically modest way Jane adds: 'Over the years I have had an enormous amount of support from countless people. Right from the early years, even from Pony Club, I had David Hunt helping me, friends and students – so many people have been there rooting for me.' But this support is no surprise, not when you know Jane; she loves horses and is so honest and caring about people. How could they not care too?

CHAPTER 6

Dressage Sidelines

LESSON FIVE · Lungeing

Traditionally lungeing has been used:

1. To prepare the young horse for the first days of being ridden.

2. To train, and build muscle tone.

3. As a means of exercise.

4. To improve the rider's position and skills.

The Spanish Riding School of Vienna is noted for expertise at lungeing. In *The Complete Training of Horse and Rider*, Alois Podhajsky wrote:

> The object of the work on the lunge is to gain the horse's confidence, make him bow to the rider's will, teach him to balance himself without a rider, and increase his proficiency. With the establishment of confidence, the foundation of obedience is laid. At the same time the horse will begin to learn the language of the aids.

Vicki Thompson integrates lungeing into the schooling of her horses to supple and strengthen them. Sometimes this schooling is for a short period prior to the ridden work; at other times it is a separate exercise in its own right. She also uses lungeing to improve and confirm the rider's position.

To quote her again: 'The establishment of a sound, solid dressage position is the

Lungeing a horse

anchor, the base which makes all good dressage possible . . . A rider who is unable to stay in balance with the horse, or unable to arrange lunge lessons should ride in walk and rising trot only and then only in easy exercises such as the transitions . . . Unbalanced riders inflict negative effects on their horses. The rider must be committed to establishing a good dressage position before "proper" dressage riding begins.'

School-lungeing is becoming popular with some trainers. For example, Ferdi Eilberg uses it to train both his young and advanced horses. With the young horses he often favours a running rein because this tends to encourage them to loosen and stretch down in a 'long and low' way so that the top line muscles are developed.

The international dressage trainer Paul Fielder has developed a unique way of lungeing. It takes the horse from an initial assessment stage through to engagement, collection and extension. His method is called 'balanced lungeing'. First, he assesses the horse by lungeing from the cavesson. He observes how the horse

Lungeing the horse
in running reins

balances himself and notes the following points: How does he balance himself in walk, trot and canter? Is each gait rhythmical? Does he hollow his back? Is he stiff? Is he strong? Powerful? Spooky or unflappable? Is he accepting the bit? How has he developed in his hindquarters, back, belly, loins and neck? Accumulating this knowledge about a particular horse enables the handler to make sensible decisions about lungeing to the best advantage.

Paul explains further: 'Balanced lungeing trains the horse in an advanced outline in the working or medium gaits. The horse works through his back, lifts his head and neck and automatically balances himself into this advanced outline. Try this exercise: imagine a line drawn from the point of the horse's hip, through the point of the shoulder to his chin. Lunge the horse and keep him balanced by maintaining his position on this imaginary line. You will notice that he automatically distributes more weight on his quarters, lightens his forehand and his gaits become more expressive. If his chin drops below this line it tends to move the horse forwards but also downwards. This plops him onto his forehand and "freewheels" him onto his hindquarters. You may mistakenly believe he is engaged when, in fact, he is avoiding taking the weight over the hind legs.'

He continues, 'The modern trend of loosening the horse with his head and neck "long and deep" has many benefits and many dangers. Balanced lungeing works the same muscles as the "long and deep" method but because the horse is

Paul Fielder
assessing a horse
for his method of
Balanced Lungeing

Balanced
Lungeing trains
the horse in an
advanced outline
in the working
and medium gaits

For Balanced Lungeing, imagine a line drawn from the point of the horse's hip through the shoulder to the chin

working in self-carriage, the negative effects of dumping the horse onto his fore-hand do not occur. The purpose of balanced lungeing is to say, "I'm the trainer, I'm the balance and I want to be able to bring the horse's hocks more under his body and lighten his forehand".'

Paul takes lungeing a step further. He describes it as lungeing to educate. He says 'The skilled trainer understands when to put the pressure on a horse and when to take the pressure off . . . The trainer is being proactive and not reactive.' And he advises students: 'Progress your trainer skills by harmonising with the horse and, particularly, avoiding conflicts. These can arise because you are making too severe demands on the horse. Go with his natural energy and gradually build on it by developing his muscles and fitness. Once you have reached a reasonable level of harmony there will be times when you should take a more passive role and allow the horse to continue his work without interference. This period of work is called "conditioning the horse". It is important because it promotes ssubmission, confidence and strength in the horse.'

Paul understands that lungeing can develop a horse both physically and mentally and his methods are designed to work with Nature and not against it. His method of balanced lungeing is expounded in *All About Lungeing* (Fielder and Hillsdon), J.A. Allen 1999.

LESSON SIX · The Spanish Way – Work In-Hand

Generally speaking, work in-hand has lain idle since the days of the great Masters of bygone centuries. Spain and Portugal prove the exceptions to this rule, most notably the Classical School in Jerez. The Spanish integrate it into all the training and start the horse's education with lateral work in-hand. Peter Maddison-Greenwell has studied Spanish dressage for many years. He explains some of their ways: 'They have a different attitude towards the horse. Most males are kept entire,

Peter Maddison-Greenwell riding the Spanish walk

and most ridden horses are stallions. From the first steps of training, the dos and don'ts of behaviour must be imprinted into the teaching language. Work in-hand establishes this control. "Getting the blood up" is another aspect of training the Spanish Way. For example, in the piaffe the horse is ridden so lightly that when an extra flash of energy is asked for it is granted without reserve. The effect is like steam escaping from a boiling kettle – turn up the heat and the steam increases – leave it alone and it slowly diminishes. It is a way of training that feels for the way of going of the horse rather than relying on technicalities. The rider 'feels' into the horse's nature and asks him to rise to the occasion and give of his best.'

Peter Maddison-Greenwell was so enthralled with Spanish training that in 1988 he and Danielle Lawniczak created El Caballo de España, the first Spanish display team in Britain. They have featured in national newspapers and on television and have performed at shows such as Royal Cornwall, Royal Windsor, Broadgate Arena and the Horse of the Year Show – on some occasions with over 10,000 spectators.

An insight into 'getting the blood up' is given by Sally O'Connor. In her book *Common Sense Dressage*, she writes about watching the late Portuguese Maestro, Nuno Oliviera.

In the Grand Prix test, ten to twelve steps of piaffe are required; that's not that many. I once had the opportunity of watching Nuno Oliveira schooling a talented young stallion who was gifted far beyond the average in the piaffe. Going across the centre of the school, he put the horse into a piaffe at X. I was chatting to another student beside me in the gallery and happened to glance at my watch. The piaffe continued, the horse lifting diagonal pairs of legs and champing softly on the bridle with the reins stretched and relaxed. I glanced again at my watch fifteen minutes later: the piaffe was still in place. The horse was relaxed, stepping even higher than before. I shall never forget that moment; it represents the ultimate mastery of the piaffe. At the end, the horse was certainly wet with exertion, but his mind remained calm throughout.

STARTING THE HORSE

First, the horse must be taught politeness in the company of other horses, and most importantly must learn respect for the handler. This is normally not difficult because the Spanish horse has such a good temperament. He is shown these new aspects of his life by 'control' work in-hand, which entails being led from a *serreta*. This is similar to a lungeing cavesson except stronger, the nosepiece being made of finely serrated metal covered in leather. For this reason the *serreta* must be used with skill and care. After a few days of 'control' leading, lungeing work begins, and within a few days of this, the first stages of work in-hand starts.

Lungeing

Peter Maddison-Greenwell explains, 'Lungeing in Spain differs from other lungeing methods. It gets the horse's blood flowing, gets him free and enjoying his work, and through this attitude the freshness of his gaits develops. He is sent a little faster than he wants to move – this forwardness must become distilled into his psyche – forwards, forwards and forwards . . . and once he becomes balanced more elevation is added. The *serreta*, lunge line and whip are used. Normally, contact with the bit is taught through the feel of the rider's hands. Moments of flexion are asked for, the horse being flexed to the inside by the handler pointing the lunge whip towards the inside shoulder. This pushes his body out on a very slightly larger circle and bends his head more to the inside. The flexions are never demanded continuously but are more moments of feeling for the bend through the free forward movement. Throughout the duration of the dressage training lungeing is practised, generally before in-hand or ridden work.'

Starting the Ridden Work

Spain's way of training empathises with the hot temperament of its horses. Peter explains, 'The moment the rider sits in the saddle, the horse must be calm. The rider progresses through the first twelve months quietly and is especially careful not to create too many resistances or problems. Any confrontations that arise should be sympathetically handled; misbehaviours are promptly and fairly sorted out.

'Walk is the mother of all gaits. The Spanish believe that there is much to be learnt from walk. In Spain the horses are exercised a lot in walk, particularly in the lateral work. The horse is loosened-up in walk, his muscles are not spoilt by demanding too much too soon. From the lungeing work the horse learns for-wardness, but when he is ridden he is kept slow, but this forwardness becomes part of his way of thinking and the slowness is more a way of calmness than lack of forward momentum. The Spanish horse has the gift of natural energy.

'After a short time of introductory lungeing and in-hand schooling with the *serreta,* the bit is introduced, but the horse is not ridden solely in the bit for some time. When this time arrives the rider uses the *serreta* reins as the bridle reins and only applies the bridle reins when the horse starts to savour the bit. Steadily, the rider's hands ask the horse to meet the bit, and the *serreta* is dispensed with and the horse is ridden solely on the bit'

TECHNIQUES FOR WORK IN-HAND

Some handlers have a feel for it. Every person, every horse, has rhythm within themselves and work in-hand releases these rhythms to the consciousness of the trainer. Work in-hand is right when it feels right. The horse should enjoy it and if he does not, it indicates there may be something wrong. 'Handlers new to the movements, such as shoulder-in, must know how to ride them before trying this work in-hand. Also, they should get help from an experienced instructor before attempting any of the difficult movements such as the piaffe or Spanish walk. Ironically, the best way to learn work in-hand is to practise. Its major advantages are:

1. The handler can observe the horse and see how he moves.

2. Physically, the handler works close to the horse and this direct connection means mistakes can be seen and corrected quickly.

3. The handler can observe how the horse is performing in comparison to perfect examples of the movements. For example, is the shoulder-in three- or four-track?

4. The handler moves in harmony with the horse, feeling, watching and observing and this helps to foster his natural talents.

5. The horse learns to view the whip as an aid and not a weapon.

6. In-hand work gymnastically exercises and prepares the horses for the task of carrying the rider.

7. The handler can keep a check on the horse's balance.

8. It is excellent for building trust between the horse and trainer.

The basic in-hand exercises are 1. forwards, 2. stop, 3. circles, 4. turn on the forehand, 5. shoulder-in, 6. travers and 7. half-pass. Some of the more advanced movements are the piaffe (occasionally a trainer teaches the passage), the Spanish walk and airs above the ground such as the levade. Most work in-hand is practised in walk. For those who want to teach it without following all the Spanish traditions I suggest they use the bridle and lunge cavesson instead of the *serreta*. A dressage whip is also needed. Stand level with the horse's shoulder, or girth.

ABOVE Levade in-hand

RIGHT Travers in-hand

(This directing spot varies with each horse and is the "move forwards" position. In front of the shoulder is the "stop" position.) The combination of hand, whip and body position aids tells the horse what to do. First, lift the reins over the horse's head (in this example the horse is on the left rein - see photograph). The outside rein lies snugly by the withers and is held in the right hand, keeping a consistent contact. The whip is also held in the right hand so that it can rest horizontally over the horse's stomach and buttocks. The left rein has a lighter, looser feel and is held in the left hand. The handler's body acts as an "inside leg". The whip can be applied with light touches on different parts of the horse's body for different effects: for example tapping the hocks, or below, asks for a sideways step; on the quarters, or the tail, activates and lowers the hindquarters; on the withers lifts the shoulders a little; on the chest asks the horse to flex his knees in a more vertical way. The whip can press gently and constantly against his body or be applied in short taps in time with the horse's rhythm. If the handler is inexperienced, or not sure how the horse will react, the hand can be used instead of the whip. There are no hard-and-fast rules regarding how to use the whip, but it must never be used to frighten the horse. He must understand that the whip aids are instructions, not punishments.'

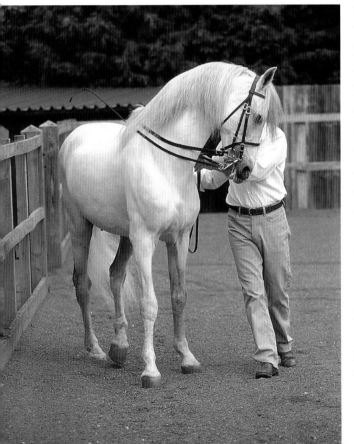

Shoulder-In

'Once the horse understands the basics, lateral work can begin. (The basics are use of the handler's body to position the horse, the whip and rein aids and forwards, stop and circle work). Position the shoulder-in by starting a small circle. Flex the horse's head to the inside and move his quarters away. The shoulders are kept in a straight line and positioned to the inside line of a circle. The whip and the outside rein control how the horse steps sideways. The shoulder-in is taken off the circle and along the track by the handler starting to walk down the line of the track, and the best place to begin this is at the point where the

Peter Maddison-Greenwell demonstrates shoulder-in in-hand

circle meets the track. Because the horse is moving with the trainer he will continue in shoulder-in on the track because this is what he has been taught to do through the basic in-hand work and because he has been positioned to move forwards and sideways. At first he may only be able to make a few steps of shoulder-in, but with quiet practice he will improve and will soon be performing shoulder-in along the whole length of the arena.'

There is such a renaissance for the Spanish horse. His bloodlines have been protected and preserved through the courage and foresight of fifteenth-century Carthusian monks. Spanish horse genes trace to many breeds: for example, the Appaloosa, the Thoroughbred, the Friesian, the Frederiksborg, the Kladruber, the Connemara, the Cleveland Bay and the Lipizzaner. But why this revival? Perhaps it is the horse's natural joie de vivre that echoes from the bluest Spanish skies, sparking romantic memories in the heart of every rider.

The Spanish horse – look into his eye and see his fire

CHAPTER 7

Cultivating Brain Power

Correct thinking is essential to good dressage: and in the process of such thinking, the individual acquires so much self-knowledge. Dressage training is a blend of brain and muscle power – quite a bubbling champagne of talents – but the greatest feat is freeing the mind. Keeping an open mind is like hopping over landmines and just praying you'll escape, and knowing that many routes lead nowhere – or even to disaster!

But let us be positive. Let us suppose that you dismiss those inherently human traits of dogma and ego, not allowing them to sneak into your dressage day! Be careful, slip from that liberated thinking for a moment, and you'll be on your way down an avalanche into another pit of self-deception and confusion!

Realistically, we are all human; we all make mistakes and only by accepting this truth can we learn from our mistakes and progress. Fundamentally, we must be brave enough to make mistakes and intelligent enough to acknowledge and correct them. Advancing from the basics, you may come to that time when you ride Grand Prix and understand a lot about dressage, but you are still in the learning process. To go further you have to be challenged, either in competition, in training, physically and/or intellectually. To originate your own ideas or to question accepted training methods requires wisdom, technical expertise and great bravery.

To test your brain power consider this – for over a decade a debate has raged between two respected dressage trainers and writers: Charles Harris and Sylvia Loch. The differences of opinions are:

1. What is the correct dressage position?

2. Precisely, how should the rider sit on and maximise the effects of the seatbones?

3. How do riders ensure they are always sitting *with* the horse, for example in turns and circles?

In the great debate both Charles' and Sylvia's viewpoints are discussed and also those of other trainers. So readers, let your minds switch to open-gear and read on! Let the words speak for themselves . . .

LESSON SEVEN · The Classical Dressage Seat of the Spanish Riding School as described by Charles Harris

Charles Harris became sworn forever to uphold the purity of dressage as practised at the Spanish Riding School of Vienna. He remembers being bonded by these principles after staying with the late Commandant of the School, Colonel Alois Podhajsky and his wife Verena. (Charles was the first, and to-date, only British rider to complete the School's full three-year graduation course (1948–1951).

Charles says: 'On leaving Poddy [Charles refers to Colonel Podhajsky in this affectionate way] he took me by the hand and made me promise, that in return for what he and the School had done for me, I would without fear or favour support the principles and fundamentals of Classical horsemanship, and that this should be based on my theoretical knowledge, practical skill and experience gained at the School. I swore faithfully never to be afraid to tell the truth; I have kept this promise, and will continue to do so.'

Charles says 'The purpose of the Classical seat, as taught by the School, is to give the rider the greatest independence, stability and balance in the saddle. This Classical seat is a posture which ensures maximum safety for the rider in the three gaits (walk, trot and canter) on both reins and all directions.' He explains further, 'It is the flesh on the rider's buttocks, i.e. the gluteous maximus, and the inner musculature of the thighs, combined with the correct upright posture of the upper part of the body, which provides the mechanism for the rider to correctly absorb the movement of the horse.

'The seat is maintained, balanced, and anchored by the pressure of the three-point skeletal action on the saddle. The pressure from these three stabilising points can be varied in numerous ways to aid the horse according to his standard of training, and help the rider according to his requirement, i.e. lighter seat, heavier seat, weight to the outside, weight to the inner-side, weight a little to the front, weight a little to the rear, etc. The coccyx is used as the sensitive "third point" balancing sensor.

'However, there are times, for example in the training of the young horse, when the rider's two seatbone contact will suffice'. However Charles warns, 'Other than in these particular instances, any rider adopting the two seatbone posture (also known as the "fork" or "crotch" posture) will find it physically impossible to use the braced back correctly in all its various Classical riding nuances. This is only possible when maximum body weight is placed and maintained on the saddle through the buttocks.'

Charles scorns modern lapses in technique, saying, 'The terms "crotch" and "fork" were never used while I was at the Spanish Riding School, except as terms of derision! None of these seat positions formed any part of the training of Classical riders in my time at the Spanish Riding School.'

He points to the words of the famous Maximilian von Weyrother, one of the Spanish Riding School's most celebrated and talented riders:

The points of contact, or the rider's base of support, must be sought in the skeleton; since the entire trunk needs to be supported, this can only be accomplished by solid parts. There are only three bones in the human skeleton which can support the rider's trunk on horseback: the seatbones and the coccyx, which is the bottom end of the spine. Unlike the seatbones, the coccyx cannot be in immediate contact with the saddle: it is higher than the seatbones, positioned centrally behind them; since, however, the coccyx is supported by the rider's buttocks, it has indirect contact with the saddle. For the rider to be in equilibrium, the line of gravity must fall between the three points of contact; the trunk should therefore be carried in such a way that the position of all its parts ensures that the line of gravity falls into the rider's base. The distance between these three points, which forms the actual support of the trunk, cannot be changed; the seatbones are the lowest ends of the pelvis, and the coccyx is fused with the pelvic girdle via the sacrum.

(In 1810 Maximilian von Weyrother was teaching horsemanship at the Austrian Military Academy and in 1814 he joined the Spanish Riding School, becoming the Commandant and Director of both Court Riding Schools. His influence still lives on and he is responsible for Directives still in use at the School today.)

Charles further argues his point by quoting Colonel Podhajsky in his book *The Complete Training of Horse and Rider*:

Both seatbones should rest firmly in the saddle so that the coccyx points to the centre line of the saddle. The seat should be open and not be pinched together in order to allow the rider to sit as deep as possible in the saddle. Both seatbones resting in the saddle, together with the coccyx, which does not touch the saddle, form the 'Triangle Of The Seat' mentioned in many old books about riding.

Charles argues for the Classical seat and using the 'third' seatbone, the coccyx, as a balancing agent and against Sylvia Loch's ideas of sitting more on the two ischia (seatbones). Charles says, 'The body weight, when placed over the two seatbones as in the fork or crotch seat, draws the rider's upper body in front of the vertical, particularly when the horse is moving. This fork seat weakens and reduces the rider's contact with the horse. Obviously this imbalance can easily disturb the rider's balance in the saddle and consequently the horse's balance. Rider and horse are not moving as one integral partnership.'

He gives advice about riding circles and changes of direction: 'The rider sits square to the front while riding the horse on straight lines. On circles and arcs, without any form of movement, turning or twisting the body, the rider is already correctly positioned and sitting square to axis.' He adds, 'Remember, it is the horse who bends, curves, or flexes his body to the arc, not the rider. If the rider in any way attempts to twist his spine (which makes it physically impossible to use the bracing of the back in any way whatsoever) he will not have the benefits of a stable "square to axis" seat. The Classical seat keeps the rider correctly balanced with the horse. (Square to axis is where the rider's shoulders are placed parallel over and above the hips and both in direct line to the axis/pivot/centre point of the circle irrespective of the diameter of the circle, or whether it is a simple circle or a pirouette.)'

In an article for *Horse and Hound* (1979), Charles stated:

When all postural faults are overcome and the rider has learnt to master the correct posture (on the lunge, without reins and stirrups) it becomes uncomfortable, and almost impossible, to resort to, or fall into an incorrect posture. Once established, the good posture requires much less muscular effort, is safer and extremely efficient and effective.

(See illustrations pages 166–167 for a comprehensive explanation of rider posture.)

Charles Harris has many rungs of knowledge: he is a Fellow of the Institute of the Horse, a Fellow of the British Horse Society, and a Fellow of the Association of British Riding Schools. His books *Fundamentals of Riding* is the Association of British Riding School's official manual. Charles has also written many pamphlets, articles and books, including *Riding and Dressage* and *Riding Technique in Pictures*.

Charles gives us some words of wisdom from his book, *Fundamentals of Riding*.

'Equestrian scholarship is to possess the knowledge and skills to successfully carry out the desired requirements with the minimum of force and effort.'

'Once a rider can recognise a correct transition, the time is ripe for studying and practising the use of the braced back.'

'In horsemanship never lose heart, continually push on, with care, effort and the correct assistance you will eventually master your difficulties.'

Charles Harris's explanation of the use of the seat

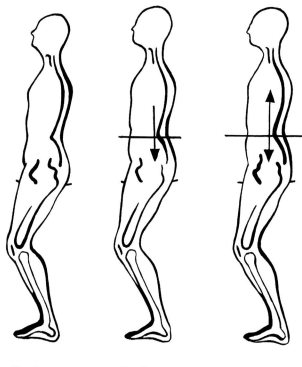

Figure 1 illustrates the 'nice' posture, but as will be seen by glancing at Figures 4 to 7 this 'nice' Figure 1 posture (Figure 1 is to clarify its limitations and not to confuse) is virtually ineffective for advanced levels of riding, the reason being that the main aids are coming from the limb extremes, i.e. hands and legs, and not from the controlling and co-ordinating mechanism of the seat and the loins.

Figure 2 Having mastered the upright posture as shown in Figure 1, the rider must now learn to sit in all variants from 'light' to 'deep' while remaining still and vertical.

Figure 3 This phase often presents problems; the learning of the 'light-above-the-waist blended with the deep seat', where the rider must seriously get to work on efficient body control. Teachers without practical experience are at a loss from this phase onwards.

Fig. 1   Fig. 2   Fig. 3

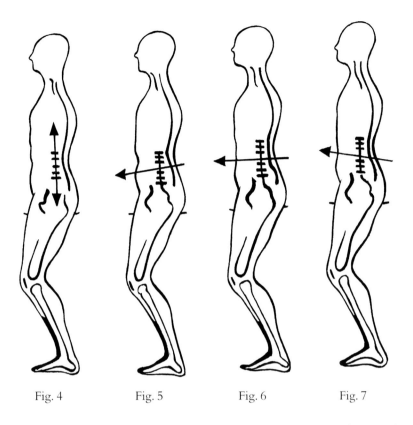

Fig. 4   Fig. 5   Fig. 6   Fig. 7

Figure 4 This demonstrates the learning of 'loin suppleness' and 'control of the loins'. A difficult exercise in which the rider learns to fully and completely absorb the motion of the horse, while retaining the upright posture and without removing the lower part of the seat from the largest contact area with the saddle.

Figure 5 This is the first phase of bracing the back – this is where the rider masters the direction and flow of his or her physical forces, *forward and downward* at one and the same time – valuable in early training of young horses. The purpose of bracing the back as explained in Figure 6, and also in Figure 7 is directly concerned with the various stages of training horses, especially for dressage.

Figure 6 The second phase of bracing the back is where the rider simultaneously directs his or her physical forces *forward and horizontally* easing/elevating the horse from

the forehand to produce a horse with a good overall balance and with efficient movement at normal gaits.

Figure 7 The third phase of bracing the back is where the rider directs his or her physical forces *forward and upward* at one and the same time. This aid acts as a stimulus towards 'elevation' and extreme collection on many planes, for example the piaffe and passage.

All that is needed to achieve a vertical posture in the saddle (as shown in Figure 1) is correct basic introductory lessons on the lunge. This should be followed by the various phases as explained in Figures 2–7. This work, correctly carried out, will give the rider maximum control with a posture of elegance and with minimum of effort, with the rider becoming an integral part of the horse in motion – bringing accolades especially needed if riders set their sights towards international dressage of the highest standards.

LESSON EIGHT · The Classical Dressage Seat of the Iberian Schools as described by Sylvia Loch

The writer Ernest Hemingway has a lot to answer for! He influenced Lord Henry Loch to move to Spain, and later Portugal to study tauromachy, the art of combat on horseback. Lord Loch began to discover the absolute necessity for the rider to be at one with the horse and he realised that the foundation for this 'oneness' came from a developed dressage seat.

Sylvia Loch's introduction to the Iberian way of riding began in 1968 when she first set foot on Portuguese soil. She says, 'I was so inspired by what I found there.' In 1971 she started training with her husband, Henry. 'I was fortunate to have become part of that system. Under Henry's guidance I learned to sit still, to think before I acted and always to listen to the horse. Riding with him, up to four or five hours a day on schoolmasters who pointed out every little fault, and then having those faults quietly explained, changed my life.'

Sylvia Loch
with Fabuloso, a
purebred Lusitano

In 1979 the Lochs moved to England and set up the United Kingdom's first Classical Academy of its kind, The Lusitano Stud and Equitation Centre; but in 1982 Lord Loch died, and Sylvia was left on her own to carry on spreading the word of the Portuguese horse and the Portuguese way of riding. She succeeded despite heavy difficulties and responsibilities and now runs an equitation centre on the Scottish Borders and writes equestrian articles and books, including *The Classical Seat* (1987).

Life is never a succession of easy movements. In the very book that proved to be a saviour lay the horns of a charging bull and soon Sylvia was smack in the middle of a controversy about the Classical dressage seat – she refers to it as the 'Bones Of Contention.'

In her book *The Classical Rider, Being At One With Your Horse* she writes:

Everyone is aware that the seat is the foundation of good riding. What people seem to forget is that no rider can hope to control their horse effectively and easily unless that foundation is established in the optimum place for the horse. It is only when the rider has sufficient suppleness and balance to drop their weight down over the horse's centre of motion, which happens also to be the horse's strongest point, around the fourteenth vertebra, that the rider can hope to achieve that magical state when they unite their balance with that of the horse. As with a seesaw controlled by one person, the key is to find the centre. Only then is the rider over the source of movement and empowered to make those small changes which can affect the entire mechanism beneath them. In riding, this can lead to remarkable improvements which will have a marked effect on the horse's continued soundness and happiness.

Driving with the seat while sitting too far back merely hollows the horse and strings him out . . . Bringing the horse's weight back involves the rider's hips coming forward and the rider sitting in the centre of the saddle and collecting the horse's energy through refined aids of the legs, seat and hands. Only from the centre can the rider use the upper body to redirect the balance.

Later in the books she adds:

Another factor which is detrimental to both the human and equine back is a seat which continuously wriggles, pushes and shoves at the horse in every stride. Such action merely upsets the horse's balance and may cause great damage in due course. All the great masters, past and present, agree it is the firm, quiet, central seat which helps the horse to come into perfect balance.

She says 'My own first experience of the three-point seat was in a Portuguese bullfighting saddle, almost identical to the manège saddle of the seventeenth and eighteenth centuries and similar in feel to the ceremonial saddles of the Spanish Riding School. No longer tilted into the chair position, the difference in contact was a revelation. Once one had got over the shock of being placed so much closer to the wither, it was an amazing experience. Suddenly one felt like a pilot instead of a passenger!'

'So why is the concept of the three-point seat so important?' Sylvia asks, and then goes on to explain: 'In the general sense, the three-point contact merely implies that the rider feels they are sitting on a full contact of the pelvic floor.' And continuing her argument, 'One author has written of the coccyx as forming the third point of the triangle, instead of the crotch. Every doctor will warn us against ever sitting on our tail bone, which is not only virtually impossible but would, of course, be excruciatingly painful. It is possible, however, to understand how such a theory came about. When one rides in the Classical three-point position there is a sensation, as one bends the small of the back forward, that one is pushing the coccyx towards the pommel at the same time. In actual fact, the coccyx is lifting well clear of the saddle as one does this, but the impression can be that the triangular feel of support stems from this point and spreads outwards and forward towards the two ischial ridges which eventually unite in front to form the fork.'

She likes the rider's position always to be compassionate towards the needs of the horse, particularly a young one. She says, 'With the youngster who is not yet sufficiently muscled through the back to begin the process of engaging his hocks or transferring weight to the quarters, the rider should adopt a more forward seat by bringing their shoulders a little in front of the vertical. This will lighten the weight in the buttocks and concentrate or deepen it more over the centre of motion and into the thighs and knees, thus ensuring non-interference with the delicate dorsal muscles which, at this stage, should work in freedom. No horse can learn to round and swing through if his back is not sufficiently made up, and this simply cannot happen if the rider has not respected those tender parts under the saddle in the early stages of schooling.'

Sylvia reiterates this sympathetic seat for the young horse in response to comments made by a contributor to a Classical Riding Club newsletter, Michael J. Stevens discussing the vertical seat. She says, 'We too often see people practising a leaning back seat (to improve the rider) at the expense of a horse who may not be physically strong enough through the back to sustain this type of exercise. Whilst some horses have really strong, well-muscled backs and loins from the age of four, others can take very little "seat" until much later, even up to seven or eight. I was pleased to hear from Mr Nico Stigt, the FEI International Dressage Judge at a seminar, that many horses would benefit at Elementary level if their riders went rising in the medium trot, instead of sitting.'

Discussing the theory of sitting square to axis she says, 'The Vienna Academy has always taught that when we ride our hips would be square to the horse's hips and our shoulders to the horse's shoulders. This is reiterated in both the German Instructor's Handbook and the British Manual of Horsemanship. This precept is a sound and important one yet, sadly, it also appears to be out of fashion among too many schools of thought.'

She continues, 'In circle work, many riders align their hips and shoulders correctly at the onset but lose the inside hip at the furthest point of the circle . . . The rider must think of solidifying the inside leg from a deep, supporting and forward inside hip to encourage curvation; only then can they feed the horse to the outside rein to complement the outside lateral stretching. It is virtually impossible for the horse to engage his inside hind leg on the circle if the rider does not mirror him.'

Sylvia lectures and teaches dressage all over the world. With four dressage books and countless magazine articles published, she is acclaimed for her contribution towards promoting sympathetic riding. In 1995 she launched the non-profit-making organisation The Classical Riding Club, her reasons being: 'To bridge the difference in attitudes and "languages" towards training the horse in a humane and dignified way. More than ever before people are not prepared to accept crude and harsh methods. We aim to create an environment where enlightened, like-minded people may come together. The Club is an organisation for the thinking rider.'

To complete her discussion on the dressage seat and to let the horse have the last word, Sylvia says, 'At the end of the day, horses are the very best judges of the truth and will tell you when or how you are going wrong. The body language of the horse gives away many clues as to how he feels the rider on his back.'

THE GREAT DEBATE: OTHER TRAINERS' VIEWS

During the 1980s the debate over the 'Triangle Of The Seat' remained in stalemate. In an effort to resolve the different opinions, Jane Kidd helped organise a seminar called 'What Do We Sit Upon?'; many experts attended, but unfortunately no finite answer evolved.

Jane is a highly respected equestrian author, journalist, editor of *British Dressage* and an International (Candidate) judge. During an interview in 1998 she said, 'We should be building common ground in dressage and not trying to find and exaggerate differences. We all have similar ultimate goals and end products, the differences, where they exist, arise in how we try to achieve those goals, but these differences are becoming less and less.

'There is much confusion as to what is "Classical". For me it means what is good and stands up to the passage of time, rather than what is "Classical". In the past even the highest levels of dressage could be cruel by our modern standards of training, for example methods were often enforced by using strong bits and sharp spurs. Today people normally aim towards good communication and compassionate methods of training and working in harmony with the horse. Perhaps even some of the best riders in the Renaissance were not "Classical" if we judge them by the modern interpretation of that term. Today we perceive "Classical" as the highest quality artistically and technically.

'Some dismiss competition riding because they see it as not standing up to Classical ideals, for example they might say the horses are trained too quickly (but great trainers like Baucher in the nineteenth century trained theirs even more quickly!) or because gadgets are used (but in the seventeenth century Newcastle created the draw reins) and although hasty training methods and/or using gadgets are suspect sometimes they were used by the greatest dressage Masters of the past, and are therefore theoretically part of "Classical" riding! I agree that competition riding is often not "Classical" because it simply is not of a good enough quality. However, at the highest competition levels standards could be viewed as *very* "Classical" on the basis that the riding and training are so superb and the whole picture is such a joy to watch.

'I believe we should bridge differences and stop looking for faults in other training methods – because all everybody really wants to achieve is to work towards excellence – and that, to my mind, is the "Classical" we should be seeking.'

To help everyday riders with their dressage position, Brigadier I. R. Prof. Kurt Albrecht of the Spanish Riding School of Vienna wrote in a letter dated 1998: 'The rider who is obliged to work on his own (that is obliged to familiarize himself in a self-taught capacity) should not be satisfied with a superficial study when it comes to familiarizing himself with the principles of the correct seat. There are many good books on the subject, though they can never be a complete substitute for practice.'

The Grand Prix rider and trainer, Paul Belasik, talks about his journey towards better dressage in his book, *Riding Towards The Light*. At the start of his journey, he felt there were many gaps in his understanding of dressage. He had studied Masters, observed and emulated top competition riders, but there was still an enormous chasm between his understanding and his ability to fine-tune to the horse.

For a while, he become over-competitive (which he believes resulted from too many pressures and stresses in his life). Paul says, 'No Master would have pushed me as I did myself. I seemed to be making progress. In spite of many flaws in posture, my seat was becoming more and more effective, more influential and more demanding . . . In order to accomplish tasks I needed a forceful intensity . . . The danger was that my will seemed to become ravenous once it tasted its own strength. It tried to control everything. With each success it became harder to control. My seat manifested this exact same force. Encounter resistance, strike it down. My seat was becoming more and more a weapon, and it began to concern me.'

Fortunately, as a consequence of a particular incident with a horse, Paul began to realise his misdirection. 'I created a din of ambition. Increased skill brought me no closer to the truth of the situation. In fact, my dominating seat became a wedge, separating me from what I really wanted. My seat became insular and demanding in that it took on a life of its own. When you are talking all the time, issuing orders, you cannot hear. Never did I just listen. Never did I just sit and feel for myself what was going on . . . hear the horse.'

Perhaps Paul encapsulates the very essence of what this chapter is all about – the ability to be humble enough to look inside yourself and see the truth. Once he had battled through his angst, Paul's riding took a turn for the better. He shares with us some of his knowledge about rider position. 'Breathing can free misguided attention – and to breathe well you must have good posture. Furthermore, only in an aware posture will you be receptive to the murmurs outside of yourself. If you are uncomfortable and tense you cannot feel. After all, riding is feeling.'

On the subject of rider position he says, 'Deep, efficient breathing helped my riding physically and psychologically. Physically, as the diaphragm muscle below the lungs contracts and flattens out, pulling fresh air into the lungs, it has the effect of compressing the organs below it. This can have the feeling of sinking the centre of gravity and internally deepening the rider's seat.' Later in his book he says: 'I could hear Dr Van Schaik's favourite phrase, "Make yourself tall". He often talked about the very natural upward growth from the abdomen to the chest which would seat the rider correctly over his seatbones.'

Paul finishes by saying, 'What I have learned is that the correct seat is never only a matter of the physique or its physical properties, even though they are essential. Many riders, even very skilful riders, never leave this plane.'

To summarise the different theories about the dressage position we might conclude that:

1. Most authorities tread along similar paths.

2. Riding is not solely a physical manifestation.

3. Riders must develop emotionally, mentally and physically before they join the ranks of good dressage riders.

4. Most importantly, flexibility and open-mindedness help to identify goals. Riders with these attitudes are much more likely to achieve their goals.

Finally, differences do exist and no clear-cut, pat answers can be conjured-up to explain them away! Developing riding techniques means discovering new truths within yourself, understanding the intricacies of long-established principles and being able to put these principles into practice.

Highways to Dressage

To understand dressage and its progression we can think of it as a highway and so travelling along the highway of dressage we pass **Junction 1** (which is the time of the Ancient Greeks and Xenophon).

Motoring on through the Ancient World, we hit a severe traffic jam, which takes two thousand, three hundred years to clear and everything about dressage grinds to a sticky halt – this is **Junction 2** (The Dark Ages).

But as we approach **Junction 3** (The Renaissance) the road clears. We change gear into an age when dressage developed as an art and lived as the ultimate war machine. Flicking into overdrive we soon pass **Junctions 4 and 5** (The establishment of the Classical Schools).

As we go past **Junction 6** (the twentieth century) we speed past changing terrains of undulating fields, forests, mountains and expanses of grasses; different roads criss-cross and some travellers get lost.

But as we spot **Junction 7** (the birth of the twenty-first century) we realise we all, eventually, pass through the same 'country' – we have arrived at our destination, a city where all knowledge from the past bubbles with the vigour of innovation and the thrusts of sports dressage.

Now Classical and Modern Schools set the standards and official sports organisations act to keep everybody on an even keel. This force moves dressage in similar directions. 'Pictures' are painted so that everybody knows what constitutes good dressage, and this knowledge is becoming more and more widely spread to different countries of the world. Today the rider understands dressage as 'making better' the horse's way of going; to go with Nature to improve the horse, but the rider also understands that this can only be to the maximum level of the individual horse's talents. These modern attitudes give a special dimension to the rider and horse relationship; both work together more. Different training methods are allowed expression and similiarities get fostered because they are proven to work best for most people and most horses. But one reality remains true – the bible of dressage will never be fully written – there will always be more chapters to add, more knowledge to be expanded upon, because this is the nature of Man, and this is the nature of dressage.

Index

Academic Equitation 10
Advanced Medium classes 124
Ahlerich **106**
aids 131-4
  cause and effect 21, 113
  consistency of 39
  leg 24, 40, 45, 131-2
  and rider's position 21-2, 150-1
  seat 23-4, 133, 166-7, 169
  simplicity of 122-3
  see also submission
Albrecht, Brigadier General Kurt
6, 172
All About Lungeing 154
Ampère 120
Anastasia **73**
Anchero 104-5
arms of rider 25
Arun Tor **97**, **105**, 106-7, *109*
Assouline, Michel 10-11, 72-3

back
  of horse 71-4, 128-30, 169-71
  of rider 23, 133, 166-7
balance
  of horse 113, 144-5
  of rider 21-3
balanced lungeing 151-4
Basic Training of the Young Horse
82-3
Baucher, François 9-10, 172
Becket *110*
Belasik, Paul 172-3
bend 87-8, 117, 131
Bertie Wooster 146
biegung 87-8
bit
  behind the bit 74
  bradoon 33, 133
  contact with see contact
  curb 133
Boldt, Harry 70, 76
Bontje, Ellen **13-14**, 70
breathing, of rider 173
Bredin, Jane 15-16
  profile of 145-9
  training principles 121-2, 145
    aids 131-4
    muscle power, connection

and balance 144-5
  simplicity 122-3
  submission 125-31
  time factors 123
  use of opposites 124-5
  working movements 134-44
breeding of horses 120
British Dressage 15
Broadstone Demonstrator 105
Broadstone Warianka **107**, *109*
Broue, Salomon de la 4, 9

Cadre Noir see Saumur Cadre
Noir
canter
  collected 34, 40, 42, 83, 117-19
  counter 35
  crookedness 87
  Elementary horse 114-15
  extended 44, 83, **105**
  Grand Prix horse 117-18
  medium 35, 44, *83*
  sequence of footfalls *83*, **84-5**
  shoulder-fore/in 46, 114, 116
  simple changes 57-8, 97
  strike-off 24
  to walk 34, 57-8, 97
  travers 52, 98
  working 40, *83*
  see also flying changes
canter pirouettes 56, **57**, 98, 118
  preparation for 56, 97-8, 114
  working movements 139-41
Cavendish, William, Duke of
Newcastle 4
centre line 39
circles 38-9, 135
  bend 87-8, 131
  inside leg to outside rein 87, 94
  inside rein 25, 38-9
  precision of 37-8
Clarke, Stephen *110*
'Classical' 66-7, 171-2
The Classical Rider, Being At One
With Your Horse 169
The Classical Riding Club 171
The Classical Seat 169
classical seat
  Charles Harris on 163-7

debate over 162-3, 171-4
  Sylvia Loch on 169-71
Clavecimbel 120
coccyx 164-5, 170
collection 41-2, 88-9
  see also individual gaits
Common Sense Dressage 156
competition dressage 65-7
  and Classical ideals 66-7, 171-2
  standards 65-6
  training for 123-4
The Complete Training of Horse
and Rider 119, 164-5
contact 81
  equal on both reins 128
  submission 125-31
  in young horse 90
  young horse 90
cooling off 79
Corder, Jean-Baptiste 10
corners 38-9, 134-5
counter-canter 35
Cumine, Anthony 146
Cumine, Susie 146, **147**
Cupido **15**, 146, 148-9
curb bit 133

Dalgety Spillers Fund 106
d'Aure, Count 10
Davison, Richard 15
de Jurenak, Kalman 74
de la Guérinière see Guérinière,
François Robichon de la
Decarpentry, General 9-10, 66-7
Demonstrator *109*
Donnerhall **68**
double bridle 132-3
downward transitions 29, 34, 57-8
d'Quino, Paolo 4
draw reins 127, **152**, 172
dressage
  competition standards 65-7
  development as sport 65
  principles 1-3
  progression of 175-6
Dressage magazine 72
Dressage Today 18
'driving' seat 169, 170-1
Du Theil, Colonel Laporte 11

durchl,,ssig 80-1, 86
Dutch Courage 110
Dutchman **63**
Duvollet, Sheila 146
Dwyer-Coles, Sarah 146

Ecole de Cavalerie 8
Eilberg, Ferdi 76, **108**
  canter pirouettes 97-9
  competition highlights *109*
  extension 96-7
  flying changes 99-101
  lateral work 92-6
  lungeing the horse 151
  piaffe and passage 101-3
  profile of 104-7
  straightening guidelines 86-8
  training highlights *110*
  training tips 103-4
  young horse's training 89-92
  see also German Scales of
Training
Eilberg, Geri 106, *110*
Eilberg, Maria 107, *110*
El Caballo de Espana 156
Elementary horse 114-16
Elementary tests 124
Enfant 62-3
extension 44-5, *82-3*, 96-7

Fabuloso **168**
Farrer, Lucy *110*
Fédération Équestre
Internationale (FEI) 19, 65-6
'feel' 70-1, 104
Fielder, Paul 151-4
figure riding 37-8
Fillis, James 131
flexion 87-8, 94-6, 130-1
flying changes 58-9, 99-101
  Elementary horse 116
  Grand Prix horse 118
  one-time 99-101, 143
  single 58-9
  working movements 141-3
fork seat 164, 165
forwardness 132
Francis, Louise 146
Fundamentals of Riding 166

gadgets, for training 172
gaits *82-3*, **84-5**
  see also individual gaits
gallop **84-5**

Garibaldi 120
German Scales of Training 75-6
  collection 88-9
  contact 81
  losgelassenheit 77-9
  rhythm 80-1
  schwung 86
  straightness 86-8
German School 67, 70, 75
Gestion Bonfire **69**
Giovanni 105, *109-10*
Goya 149
Grand Prix horse 117-19
Grand Prix test 19
Greece, ancient 3
Grisone, Federico 3-4
Guérinière, François Robichon
de la 1, 4, 8-9

hacking 103
half-halts
  Bert Rutten on 112
  Ferdi Eilberg on 91-2
  Jane Bredin on 133-4
  Vicki Thompson on 34, 37, 42
half-pass 52-3, 94-6, **115**
  assessing quality of *96*
  Elementary horse 114
  faults in 95-6
  riding *53*
  teaching the horse 52
  working movement 138-9
half-transitions 36-7, 42, 112
Handler, Colonel Hans 6
hands of rider 25, 28, 30, 132-3
Harris, Charles 163
  on the classical seat 163-7
head, position of horse's 71-4,
128-30
  in lungeing 152-4
Hendrix, Wiel 120
Hester, Carl 63
Highlander *109*
Hinnermann, Johann 76
Hiscox Askari 15
horse breeding 120
Horse and Hound 74-5
Hunt, David 145-6, 149

in-hand work 158-61
inside leg to outside rein 87, 94

Janssen, Sjef 71, 74-5, 148
  training principles 121-2

see also Bredin, Jane
Jazz Dancer 63, **119**
Jenkins, Lindsay *110*
Jensen, Ann-Grethe 67
judging, standards 65-6

Kidd, Jane 66-7, 171-2
Klimke, Dr Reiner 70, 76, 105,
106
  Basic Training of the Young Horse
82-3
Kottas, Arthur 6-8

lateral work 94-9
  development of 52-5, **56**
  Elementary horse 114
  introduction of 45
  see also individual movements
Laus, Pia 71
Lawniczak, Danielle 156
'lazy' horse 24, 40, 114, 124, 132
leg aids 24, 131-2
  extended walk 45
  'lazy' horse 24, 40, 132
leg position 24, 39, 131-2
lengthening 35, 43-4, *82-3*
  see also extension
Lette, Eric 19
levade, in hand **159**
L'Hotte, General 10
Lipizzaner horse 6-7
Loch, Lord Henry 168-9
Loch, Sylvia 16, 168-9, 171
  on classical seat 169-71
loins, suppleness **167**
'long and low' 130
  see also losgelassenheit
Lorelie Sea Hifi 62
Loriston-Clarke, Jennie *110*
losgelassenheit 77-9
Lucky Star 149
lungeing 150-1
  the advanced rider 30-5
  balanced method 151-4
  the novice rider 25-30
  in Spanish dressage 157
  trainer's skills 154

Maddison-Greenwell, Peter 155-6
Mason, Diana *110*
Meade, Richard *110*
The Method and Novel Ways of
Training Horses 4
Müseler, Wilhelm 119

Neckermann, Dr 70
Newcastle, Duke of *see*
Cavendish, William, Duke of
Newcastle
Nissan Gigolo **68**
novice rider 25-30
novice tests 123-4
Novital, Commandant de 9

O'Connor, Sally 156
Oliveira, Nuno 156
Olympic Larius **14**
open rein 25, 38-9
Ordine di Cavalcare 4
Otto-Crepin, Margit 67, 71
outline of horse 71-4, 128-30,
151-4
over-riding 80
overbending 74
overtracking *82*

Paillard, Commandant Saint Fort
72-3
Parcival 120
Parthenon stone carvings 3
passage 103, 118, 143-4
Petit Prince **13**
Phillips, Captain Mark *110*
piaffe 101-3, 118, 143-4
   introducing 59-60, 143-4
   on lunge 31, **32**
   in Spanish dressage 156
Pignatelli 4
pirouettes 54
   canter 56, **57**, 97-9, 114, 118
   walk 54, 55
   working movements 139-41
Pluvinel, Antoine de 4, 9
Podhajsky, Colonel Alois 6, 19,
163
   on lungeing 150
   on triangle of the seat 164-5
Polak, Riding Master **17**
Portuguese bullfighting saddle
170
position of rider 21-5, 150-1
   corrections 30
   guidelines 23
   and horse's balance 113
   see also seat of rider
Prince Consort *110*

Questions Equestres 10

Rehbein, Karin **68**
reins
   double bridle 132-3
   draw 127, **152**, 172
   inside 25, 38-9
   open 25, 38-9, *47*, *49*
   outside 87, 94-6
   riding without 28-9, 31, 34
relaxation, for horse 103
Rembrandt **68**
renvers 94
rest periods 118
rhythm 80-1
Richtlinien see German Scales of
Training
rider, qualities of 2-3
Riding Logic 119
Robbi 120
Rochowansky, Franz 'Rocky'
17-20, 62, **63**
Rothenberger, Sven **13**, 70
'round and deep' 71-4, 128-30
Rubens 63
rushing horse 40, 124
Rutten, Bert 20, 111
   profile of 120-1
   training an Elementary horse
114-16
   training basics 111-13
   training a Grand Prix horse
117-19
Rutten, Jo 120

Saint Antoine 4
St Cyr School 72
Saumur Cadre Noir 4, 9-12, 72
Scales of Training *see* German
Scales of Training
Schulten-Baumer, Dr Uwe 71-2,
75
Schultheiss, Willi 76
Schumacher, Conrad 12, 15-16,
67, 70-1
   on half-halts 133
schwung 86
seat aids 23-4, 133, 166-7, 169
seat bones 163-7
seat of rider 23, 133
   in circles/turns 38, 165, 171
   debate over 162-3, 171-4
   tension in 172-3
   three-point 163-7, 169-71
   in working gaits 39
   and young horse 170-1
Selles Français horse 11
serreta 156-8

Sewell, Tom 5-6
shoulder-fore 45, **93**
   canter 46, 114
   riding *47*
shoulder-in 46, 48, 92-4, **115**
   Elementary horse 114
   Grand Prix horse 117
   Guérinière on 8-9
   in hand 160-1
   riding *49*
   value of 48
   working movements 135-6
shoulders of the rider 25
simple changes 57-8, 97
sitting trot, lungeing novice rider
27
Slibovitz 71
Soldier Boy 146
Spanish dressage 155-6
   lungeing 157
   starting the horse 156-7
   starting ridden work 157-8
   work in-hand 158-61
Spanish horse 155-6, 161
The Spanish Riding School of
Vienna 1-2, 5-8, 18-19
   Chief Riders 5-6
   classical seat 163-7
   horses 6-7, 19
   lungeing 150
   qualities of the riders 7-8
*The Spanish Riding School of
Vienna* 5
Spanish walk **155**
'spring' 86
stellung 87-8
Stigt, Nico 171
straightness 86-8, 117
Stückleberger, Christine 67
submission 125-6, 130
   bending 131
   equal contact 128
   flexion 130-1
   and shape of horse 128-30
   teaching the horse 127-8

takt 80-1
Tapster **108**, 110
tempo *82*
Thompson, Mary *110*
Thompson, Vicki 20, **119**
   collecting the gaits 41-2
   direct transitions 35-6
   figure riding 37-9
   flying changes 58-9
   half-halts 37

half-transitions 36-7
lateral work development 52-6
lateral work introduction 45-52
lengthening the gaits 43-5
lungeing the advanced rider 30-6
lungeing the horse 150
lungeing the novice rider 25-30, 150-1
piaffe 59-60
position of the rider 21-5, 150-1
profile 62-4
simple changes 57-8
on trainers/training 20-1
training tips 60-2
working gaits 39-41
Thoroughbred horses 11, 16
three-point seat 163-7, 169-71
'through' 80-1, 86
tracking up 41, 82
trainers
    qualities of 2-3
    relations with rider 119
    Vicki Thompson on 20-1
    and women riders 71
training
    consistency 113
    and 'feel' 70-1, 104
    flexibility in 103
    keeping an open mind 104, 162
    of new movements 114-15
    problems 91, 113
    'ruts' 103-4
    time factors 123-4
    using opposites 124-5
transitions 35-6, 57-8, 111-12
    and canter pirouettes 56, 97
    and 'lazy' horse 114
    ridden on lunge 29, 34
    see also half-transitions
travers 50-2, 94, 137
    in canter 52
    on circle 98, 114
    in-hand **159**
    in preparation for half-pass 138
    working movement 137
trot
    collected 41-2, *83*
    Elementary horse 114, 116
    extended 44, *83*
    lengthened strides 43-4
    medium 44, *82*, 125
    sequence of footfalls 82-3, **84-5**
    working 40, *83*
turns 38-9, 87-8

under-riding 80
Understanding Equitation 73
'up and in' 74-5, 130
Uphoff-Becker, Nicole **68**, 71, 75
upward transitions 34, 114

Van Grunsven, Anky **69**, 74
Van Schaik, Dr 173
Vargas 4
Verdi 146
Vicktor 63, **64**
von Gratz, General 19
von Lohneissen, Georg Englehard 4
Von Loon, Ernest 120
von Schafer, Paul 6
von Weyrother, Maximilian 6, 164

Wahl, Georg 20
walk
    collected 41-2, *82*
    Elementary horse 114, 116
    extended 44-5, *82*
    free *82*
    Grand Prix horse 117, 119
    on a long rein 114, 116, 119
    medium 39-40, *82*
    sequence of footfalls *82*, **84-5**
walk pirouettes 54, 55
Warmblood horse 11, 67, 71
warming up 77-9
weight aids 24
Werth, Isabell **68**, 71, 75
Weyden **13**
whip
    in-hand work 160
    and leg aids 24, 40, 132
women riders 71
working deep *see* 'round and deep'
working gaits 39-41, 82-3
working movements
    corners and circles 134-5
    flying changes 141-3
    half-pass 138-9
    pirouettes 139-41
    shoulder-in 135-6
    travers 137

Xenophon 3

Yagi, Mieko *110*
young horse 61, 89-91
    and rider's seat 170-1

Zirkoon 120